WINDOWS 11

GUIDEBOOK

A simple Guide with easy instructions to master
Windows 11 effectively for Beginners and Advanced
Users

Rhyan Baisten

TABLE OF CONTENTS

INTRODUCTION

What is Windows 11?

Windows 11 is the latest operating system from Microsoft. It is designed to be easier to use, more productive, more secure, and more fun than previous versions of Windows. The design has been simplified, and the user experience empowers your productivity and inspires your creativity. It's modern, fresh, clean, and beautiful. From the new Start button and taskbar to each sound, font, and icon, everything was done intentionally to put you in control and bring a sense of calm and ease. The Start menu at the center made it easy to quickly find what you need. Start utilizes the power of the cloud and Microsoft 365 to show you your recent files no matter what platform or device you were viewing them on earlier, even if it was on an Android or iOS device.

What is the New Window Compared to the Previous Version

 Managing and switching between virtual desktops is a more seamless experience compared to Windows 10. Windows 11 offers a virtual desktop setup reminiscent of Mac, enabling you to effortlessly switch between multiple desktops for various purposes, whether it's for personal use, work, school, or gaming. Microsoft's latest operating system comes packed with a multitude of new features and enhancements when compared to its predecessors, most notably Windows 10. Here are some key distinctions between Windows 11 and Windows 10:

1. Redesigned Start Menu and Taskbar:
- It introduces a centered Start menu and taskbar, offering extensive customization options, while Windows 10 retains a left-aligned menu with fewer personalization choices.

2. Snap Assist for Multitasking:
- It debuts Snap Assist, facilitating window organization in a grid layout for efficient multitasking. In contrast, Windows 10 offers a Snap feature for window positioning, but not in a grid pattern.

3. Desktop Groups for Organization:
- It incorporates Desktop Groups, allowing users to create and seamlessly switch between distinct desktops for specific purposes (e.g., work, gaming, and personal). Windows 10 features virtual desktops but lacks predefined groupings or themes.

4. Microsoft Phone Link for Smartphone Integration:
- It presents the Microsoft Phone Link feature, enabling notifications, message reading, and call-making from your PC

using both iPhone and Android devices. Windows 10 includes the Your Phone app for Android integration but lacks support for iPhones.

5. PC Game Pass for Gaming Enthusiasts:

- It introduces the PC Game Pass, providing access to a vast library of high-quality PC games, including day-one releases, for immersive gaming experiences with friends. Windows 10 doesn't offer this feature, but Xbox Game Pass for PC is available separately.

6. Auto HDR for Gaming Visuals:

- It enhances gaming visuals with Auto HDR, enriching colors and contrast on compatible displays. Windows 10 lacks this feature but allows manual HDR activation on supported devices.

7. DirectStorage for Faster Loading Times:

- It introduces DirectStorage, significantly reducing game loading times by allowing games to directly access data from storage devices. Windows 10 doesn't incorporate this feature, although performance can be improved using SSDs or NVMe drives.

Hardware Requirement

These are the minimum hardware requirements for Windows 11:

- **Processor**: A compatible 64-bit processor or system on a chip (SoC) with a clock speed of at least 1 gigahertz (GHz) and two or more cores. The processor must also be listed among Microsoft's approved CPUs.
- **RAM**: A minimum of 4 gigabytes (GB) of RAM.
- **Storage**: A storage device with a capacity of 64 GB or more. Additional storage may be necessary to accommodate Windows 11 updates.

- **System Firmware**: Your system should support UEFI (Unified Extensible Firmware Interface), which is a modern alternative to the traditional PC BIOS. It should also be capable of Secure Boot, which may be enabled in your PC settings.
- **TPM**: Your PC must have a Trusted Platform Module (TPM) version 2.0, a security chip that enhances data and device security. You may need to enable TPM in your PC settings.
- **Graphics Card**: Your graphics card should be compatible with DirectX 12 or a later version and have a WDDM 2.0 driver.
- **Display**: A high-definition (720p) display with a diagonal size exceeding 9 inches and support for 8 bits per color channel.
- **Internet Connection and Microsoft Account**: When setting up Windows 11 Pro for personal use or Windows 11 Home, an internet connection and a Microsoft account are required. Regardless of the edition, internet access is necessary for updates and to utilize certain features.

These are the minimal hardware prerequisites. If your current PC does not meet these specifications, you may encounter difficulties when trying to install or upgrade to Windows 11. In such cases, you might want to contemplate purchasing a new PC that complies with these requirements.

FEATURES OF WINDOWS 11

Android App

Android applications on your PC, courtesy of the Amazon App Store and the updated Microsoft Store. You have the flexibility to download and install Android apps from these platforms and utilize them in conjunction with your Windows applications. Furthermore, you can conveniently pin your preferred Android apps to the taskbar or the Start menu for quick and hassle-free access.

Widgets

Widgets are compact, interactive applications that offer a diverse array of information and convenient access to useful tools directly from your desktop. These widgets are fully customizable, prioritizing speed, lightweight operation, and user-friendliness. You have the flexibility to resize and relocate them to align with your individual preferences.

Microsoft Teams

Microsoft Teams Integration: It introduces an integrated Microsoft Teams experience, enabling seamless chatting, calling, and video conferencing with your friends, family, and coworkers directly from your PC. You can easily access Teams from the taskbar or Start menu and initiate conversations with anyone in your contact list. Moreover, during a Teams session, you can share your screen, files, emojis, GIFs, and a variety of other content to enhance collaboration and communication.

Desktop

Introduces a novel Desktop functionality that empowers you to craft and switch between diverse desktop environments for specific tasks, be it work, gaming, or personal use. Each desktop can be personalized with unique wallpapers, applications, and settings to suit your preferences. You have the flexibility to transfer windows between these desktops or organize them into coherent Snap layouts. Accessing the Desktop feature is as straightforward as clicking on the Task View icon on the taskbar or pressing the Windows logo key + Tab.

Snapshot Group

Snapshot Group introduces the innovative Snap Group feature, which allows you to preserve and recover the arrangement of your open windows as you transition between different devices or monitors. For instance, if you use a laptop and an external monitor, you can organize the windows on each screen to your liking and effortlessly switch between them without losing your carefully crafted layout. Additionally, you can conveniently access your Snap Groups in the taskbar, hover over them to preview them, and promptly restore them to their previous configurations.

CHAPTER ONE

INSTALLING WINDOWS 11

Installing Via Windows Update

To determine if your device is eligible for an upgrade, follow these steps:

1. Click on the Start menu.
2. Navigate to Settings.
3. Select Update & Security.
4. Within the Windows Update section, click on Check for updates.

If Windows 11 is available for your device and you wish to proceed, simply download and install the upgrade.

Upgrading from Windows 10 to Windows 11

Upgrading from Windows 10 to Windows 11 is a simple process, but it's important to make sure your current Windows 10 installation is fully updated before you start. This ensures that everything goes smoothly and helps avoid potential issues during the upgrade.

First, you'll need to check for any available updates on your current Windows 10 system. Go to your Settings by clicking the Start menu and selecting the gear icon. Then, click on Update & Security, and select Windows Update. Once you're in the Windows Update section, click Check for Updates. This will search for any pending updates that need to be installed.

If any updates are available, make sure to install them. Some updates may require a restart of your computer, so be sure to save any important work before you begin the update process. After the restart, the updates will continue to be installed, and your system will be ready for the upgrade to Windows 11.

Once your current version of Windows 10 is fully updated, you can move forward with the upgrade to Windows 11. The process is typically quick and easy, especially if your system meets all the requirements for Windows 11. By ensuring your Windows 10 system is up to date, you're laying a solid foundation for a smooth and trouble-free upgrade.

System Requirements for Windows 11 Installation

To install Windows 11 on your PC, your device needs to meet certain minimum system requirements. If your device doesn't meet these, you might not be able to upgrade to Windows 11 and could consider getting a new PC. If you're unsure whether your current device is compatible, you can check with the manufacturer or use the PC Health Check app if your device is already running Windows 10. Keep in mind that the app doesn't check for graphics card or display compatibility, as most systems that meet the requirements will work with those as well.

Before you start the upgrade, make sure your device is running Windows 10, version 2004 or later. You can get the update through Windows Update by going to Settings > Update & Security.

Here are the specific requirements for your system:
- **Processor:** At least 1 gigahertz (GHz) or faster with 2 or more cores on a compatible 64-bit processor or a System on a Chip (SoC).
- **RAM:** 4 gigabytes (GB) or more.
- **Storage:** A minimum of 64 GB storage. Keep in mind that more storage may be needed to keep Windows 11 up-to-date.

- **System Firmware:** UEFI, Secure Boot capable. You can find information on how to check if your PC meets this requirement.
- **TPM (Trusted Platform Module):** Version 2.0. Instructions for enabling TPM on your PC can be found online.
- **Graphics Card:** Must be compatible with DirectX 12 or later and support WDDM 2.0 driver.
- **Display:** High definition (720p) display, larger than 9" diagonally, with 8 bits per color channel.

Copilot+ PC Requirements

If you're looking to use **Copilot+ PCs**—Windows 11 devices enhanced with AI capabilities, including turbocharged neural processing units (NPUs)—you'll need hardware that supports these high-performance features. These PCs are designed to handle demanding AI processes, such as real-time translation and image generation, performing over 40 trillion operations per second (TOPS).

Along with meeting the basic Windows 11 requirements, Copilot+ PCs need the following:

- **Processor:** A compatible processor or **SoC** with an NPU that can perform 40+ TOPS, such as:
    - **AMD Ryzen™ AI 300 series**
    - **Intel® Core™ Ultra 200V series**
    - **Snapdragon® X**
    - **Snapdragon® X Plus**
    - **Snapdragon® X Elite**
- **RAM:** 16 GB DDR5/LPDDR5.
- **Storage:** 256 GB SSD/UFS.

Using the Installation Assistant to Install

To utilize the Installation Assistant and seamlessly install the operating system, follow these steps:

1. Visit the Windows 11 Downloads page and click Download now under the Installation Assistant section.
2. This action will provide you with an executable file for the Windows 11 Installation Assistant, and the installation will commence immediately upon execution.
3. After reviewing the terms of the agreement, click Accept and install.
4. The tool will then assess your device's compatibility with Windows 11 and proceed to download the necessary files. The duration of this process may vary based on your internet speed and device performance.
5. Once the download is completed, the tool will prompt you to restart your device to initiate the installation. Ensure that you save any ongoing work and close all applications before proceeding with the restart.
6. Following the restart, the tool will continue the installation process, displaying progress indicators. It's crucial not to power off your device or interrupt the installation at this stage.
7. Upon completion of the installation, you will be welcomed by the new Windows 11 setup screen. Simply follow the provided instructions to finalize the setup and embark on your new Windows 11 experience.

How to perform a clean installation with Windows 11

A clean installation involves installing the operating system on a computer that lacks any prior Windows version or existing data. This process is beneficial for those seeking a fresh start, erasing all hard drive content, or addressing issues hindering Windows' proper operation. To perform a clean installation with Windows 11, you'll need the following:

1. **A Compatible Computer**: Ensure your computer meets the minimum system requirements for Windows 11. You can verify compatibility using the PC Health Check app or by visiting the official Microsoft website.

2. **8 GB or Larger USB Flash Drive**: This is necessary to create a bootable installation media. You can utilize the Media Creation Tool to download and prepare the installation media on the USB drive.

3. **Backup of Important Files**: Given that the installation process erases everything on your hard drive, safeguard your crucial files and data by creating a backup. You can use an external hard drive, a cloud service, or another storage device for this purpose.

Once you've gathered these prerequisites, follow these steps for a clean installation:

1. Insert the USB flash drive with the installation media into your computer and restart it. You might need to adjust the boot order in your BIOS or UEFI settings to boot from the USB drive. Refer to your computer manufacturer's website or user manual for guidance.

2. When the Windows logo appears, press any key to initiate the setup process. Select your language, time, and keyboard preferences, then click Next.

3. Click Install now and enter your product key if you have one. If you lack a product key or are reinstalling the same Windows edition you had previously, choose I don't have a product key and select your edition later.

4. Accept the license terms and click Next. Opt for Custom: Install Windows only (advanced) as the installation type.

5. Choose the drive where you intend to install Windows 11 and click Next. If you have multiple drives or partitions, exercise caution while deleting them to create a single large drive for Windows 11, as this action cannot be reversed.

6. Allow the installation process to proceed. Your computer may reboot several times during this phase. Avoid shutting down your computer or interrupting the installation.

7. After the installation concludes, you'll encounter the initial setup screen. Here, you can customize settings, establish a user account, and sign in with a Microsoft account if desired. Follow the on-screen instructions to complete the setup and embark on your fresh Windows 11 experience.

What you should know before Installing Windows 11 on Non –Supported Devices

Installing Windows 11 on non-supported devices is not recommended by Microsoft, as it may cause compatibility issues, security risks, and performance problems. However, if you are determined to try Windows 11 on your device, you should know the following things before you proceed:

- You should back up your important data before installing Windows 11, as everything on your hard drive will be erased during the installation process. You can use an external hard drive, a cloud service, or another device to store your backup.
- Create Bootable Installation Media: Begin by preparing a bootable installation medium, using a blank USB flash drive with a minimum storage capacity of 8 GB. The Media Creation Tool is a helpful resource for downloading and creating this installation media on the USB drive. This bootable media will be indispensable for your Windows 11 installation.
- Configure UEFI Firmware Settings: Adjust specific settings within your device's UEFI firmware (Unified Extensible Firmware Interface) to enhance compatibility with Windows 11. These settings typically include enabling TPM 2.0, Secure Boot, and transitioning to the GPT (GUID Partition Table) partition scheme. For comprehensive instructions, refer to your device manufacturer's website or consult your user manual.
- Apply Registry Hacks (with Caution): In certain instances, you may need to employ registry hacks to circumvent compatibility checks and compel Windows 11 to install on your device. These hacks entail modifying registry editor values and creating specific files within the installation media. While detailed steps can be found on various websites, exercise extreme caution to avoid errors or system damage during this process.

Please note that attempting to install Windows 11 on unsupported hardware carries inherent risks, and it's essential to exercise caution and thoroughly research each step to ensure a smooth installation without compromising your system's integrity.

Installing Windows in an Unsupported Device

To install Windows 11 on unsupported hardware using a USB drive and ISO file for a clean installation, follow these steps:

1. Create a bootable USB drive using a third-party tool like Rufus or Command Prompt.
2. Ensure that your device can boot from a USB drive by adjusting the UEFI settings. As these settings may vary across different computers, refer to your manufacturer's support website for specific instructions.

Here's how to proceed with the installation:

1. Insert the Windows 11 USB flash drive into the unsupported PC.
2. Boot the computer from the USB drive by pressing any key when prompted.
3. Once the setup begins, press Shift + F10 on your keyboard to open Command Prompt.
4. In the Command Prompt window, enter the following command and press Enter:
5. The Setup will open the Registry Editor (regedit).
6. Navigate to the following path in the Registry Editor:
   HKEY_LOCAL_MACHINE\SYSTEM\Setup
7. Right-click the Setup folder key, select New, and then choose the Key option.

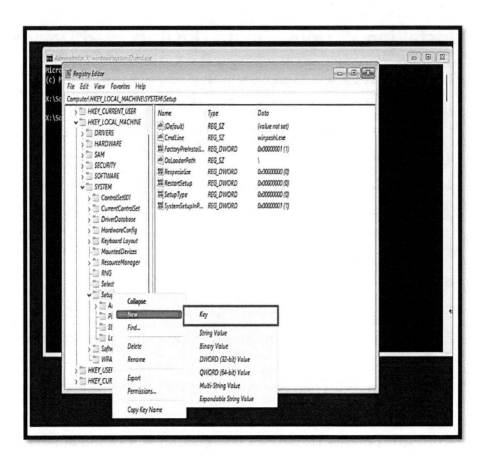

8. Name the newly created key LabConfig and press Enter.
9. Right-click the LabConfig folder key, select New, and then choose the DWORD (32-bit) Value option.
10. Name the new DWORD key BypassTPMCheck and press Enter.
11. Double-click the BypassTPMCheck key you just created.
12. Change its value by Double-clicking the newly created key and setting its value from 0 to 1.

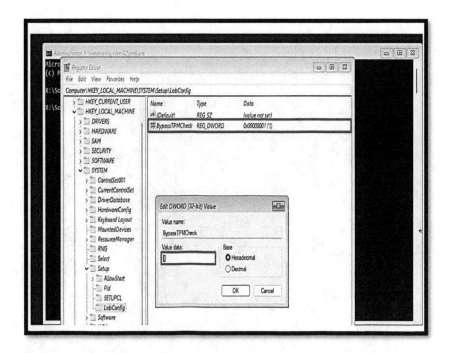

13. Click the OK button to save the changes.

14. Click the Next button.

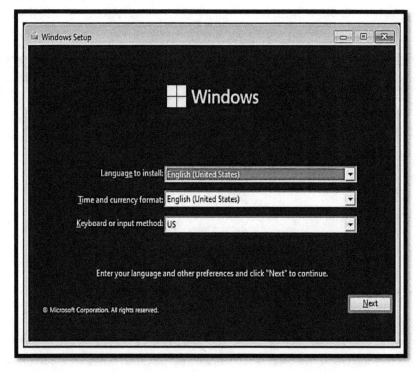

15. Click the Install Now button.

16. Click the I don't have a product key option if you are reinstalling. If Windows 11 has been previously activated after the installation, reactivation will happen automatically.

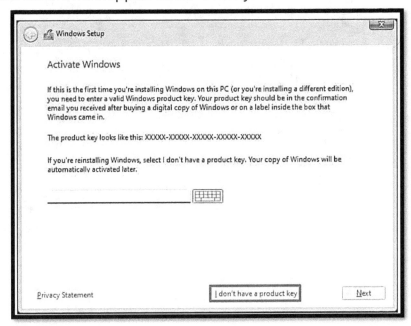

17. Select the edition of Windows 11 that your license key activates (if applicable).

18. Check the I accept the license terms option.

19. Click the Next button.

20. Select the Custom: Install Windows only (advanced) option.

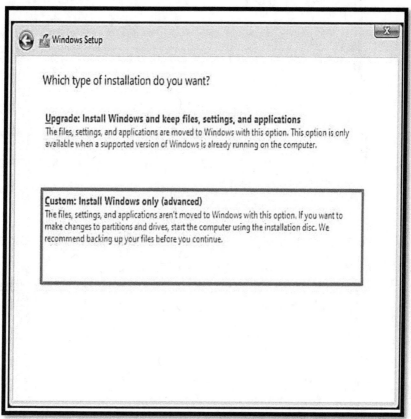

21. Select each partition in the hard drive you want to install Windows 11 and click the Delete button. (Typically, the Drive 0 is the drive that contains all the installation files.)

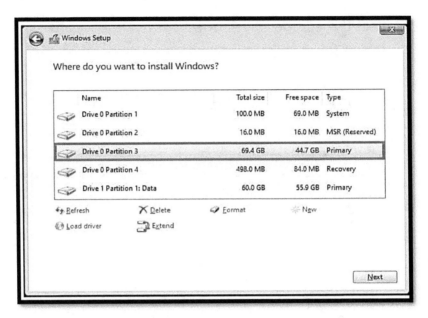

Warning: Deleting a partition also deletes all data on the drive. Also, it is not required to delete the partitions from a secondary hard drive.

22. Select the hard drive (Drive 0 Unallocated Space) to install Windows 11 on an unsupported device.

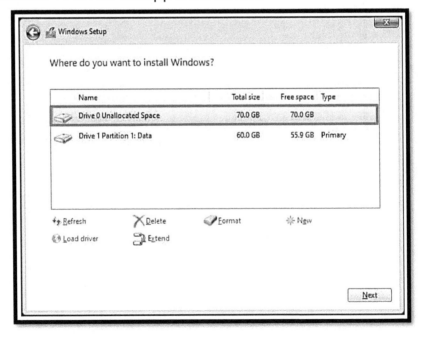

23. Click the Next button.

24. Select your region setting after the installation on the first page of the out-of-the-box experience (OOBE).

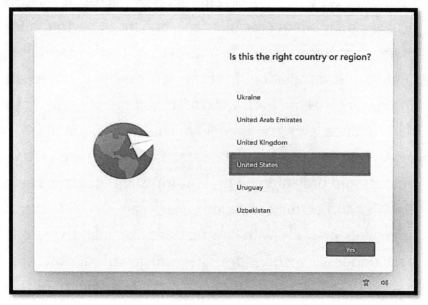

25. Click the Yes button.

26. Select your keyboard layout setting.

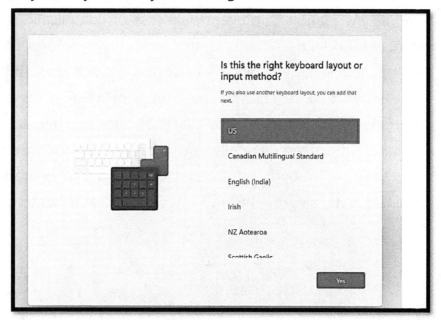

CONCLUSION

The installation represents a significant step forward in the world of operating systems. This new iteration of Microsoft's flagship OS offers a sleek and modern user interface, enhanced performance, and a host of new features designed to improve productivity and user experience. During the installation process, it's essential to ensure that your computer meets the system requirements to ensure optimal performance and compatibility. The installation itself has become more user-friendly over the years, with Microsoft streamlining the process and providing helpful prompts and guidance along the way.

Once is successfully installed, users can enjoy a fresh and visually appealing interface, with new features like Snap Layouts, Widgets, and a revamped Microsoft Store. The inclusion of support for Android apps through the Microsoft Store is a notable addition, further expanding the ecosystem and utility of Windows 11.

However, as with any major OS update, it's crucial to back up your data before installation to prevent data loss or complications during the process. Additionally, ensure that your software and hardware are compatible with Windows 11 to avoid potential compatibility issues. The installation can bring significant benefits in terms of improved performance, features, and user experience. By following the installation process carefully and taking necessary precautions, you can make a smooth transition to this modern operating system, unlocking its full potential and enjoying all that it has to offer.

CHAPTER TWO

CONFIGURING AND CUSTOMIZING WINDOWS

Initial Look and Feel Compared to Windows 10

The equivalent mode in Windows 11 closely resembles the default desktop experience, albeit with a slightly enlarged taskbar. The Start Menu maintains its original size. Since only a small percentage of users employed Windows 10 for its tablet-oriented experience, the shift back to a more conventional desktop setup in Windows 11 is unlikely to cause any significant inconvenience to most users.

Windows 11 introduces a fresh design, notably featuring a centered Start menu and Taskbar. This update brings a new interface that bears a resemblance to macOS, characterized by its sleek design, rounded corners, and soft pastel color scheme. Notably, the iconic Start menu has been relocated to the center of the screen, giving the operating system a distinct look.

Using Windows – Programs and the Start Menu

How to open and Manage Applications

To open an application, select the Start icon (which is in the center) and then click on the app you want to launch. You can also use the search bar at the top of the Start menu to find an app by typing its name or a keyword. To see all your installed apps, you can click on the All Apps button at the top right corner of the Start menu. You can also pin your favorite or frequently used apps to the Start menu by right-clicking on them and selecting Pin to Start. To unpin an app, right-click on it again and select Unpin from Start

How to Remove Unwanted Applications from Your Computer

How to Uninstall Unwanted Applications from Your Computer: If you wish to remove an application that is no longer needed or used on your computer, you can do so by following these steps:
1. Open the Start menu and select Settings (the gear icon).
2. Navigate to the Apps section on the left side and then click on Apps & features on the right.
3. Locate the application you want to uninstall and click on the three dots next to it.
4. Choose Uninstall and confirm your decision.

Alternatively, you can also right-click on an app in the Start menu or the All Apps list and select Uninstall.

Remove programs from the Start menu.

Removing App Icons from the Start Menu is a straightforward process. Just follow these steps:

1. Click on the Start button located in the center of the taskbar.
2. Scroll through the list of pinned applications in the Start menu until you locate the app you want to remove.
3. Right-click on the app you wish to remove and choose 'Unpin from Start.'

How to use the start screen menu in Windows 11

The Start Screen Menu is a functionality that enables you to interact with widgets, which are compact windows displaying personalized information like weather, news, stocks, sports, and more. Accessing the Start Screen Menu can be done through several methods:

1. Click on the Widgets icon located in the taskbar (adjacent to the Search icon).
2. Swipe from the left edge of the screen.
3. Alternatively, use the Windows + W keyboard shortcut.

You have the flexibility to put your widgets as per your preferences. This includes adding or removing widgets, resizing or repositioning them, and adjusting their settings.

Customizing the Windows Start Menu and Taskbar

To personalize the Start menu, follow these steps:

1. Launch the Settings app (by pressing the Windows key + I).
2. Navigate to Personalization > Start.
3. Here, you'll find a handful of customization options. You can add, rearrange, or remove pinned apps directly within the Start menu. Additionally, you have the choice to completely replace the Start menu with an alternative design or revert to the classic Start menu if you prefer.

Restore the Classic Start Menu.

Reverting to the Classic Start Menu is possible, but it's worth noting that this method isn't officially supported by Microsoft and may not be compatible with all Windows 11 builds. To attempt this customization, follow these steps:

1. Open the Registry Editor (regedit.exe).
2. Navigate to HKEY_CURRENT_USER\Software\Microsoft\Windows\CurrentVersion\Explorer\Advanced.
3. Create a new DWORD value with the name Start_ShowClassicMode and set its data to 1.
4. After making this change, restart your computer, and you should see the familiar old-style Start menu.

If you wish to return to the default Windows 11 Start menu:

- Either delete the Start_ShowClassicMode value you created, or
- Change its data back to 0.

How to customize the start screen

The Start Screen is a powerful feature that allows you to interact with widgets, which are compact windows displaying personalized information such as weather, news, stocks, sports, and more. Here's how you can put your Start Screen experience:

1. Access the Start Screen by clicking on the Widgets icon located in the taskbar (next to the Search icon), swiping from the left edge of the screen, or using the convenient Windows + W keyboard shortcut.
2. Once on the Start Screen, you have the flexibility to customize your widgets in various ways. You can add or remove widgets, resize them, rearrange their placement, and fine-tune their settings according to your preferences.

Pinning Applications to the Taskbar

To pin apps to the taskbar, you can follow these steps:

1. Click on the Start button, then scroll to the app you want to pin.
2. Press and hold (or right-click) the app icon.
3. From the menu that appears, select 'More,' and then choose 'Pin to taskbar.'

If the app is already open on the desktop, you can also pin it to the taskbar by:

1. Pressing and holding (or right-clicking) the app's taskbar icon.
2. Selecting 'Pin to taskbar' from the context menu.

Pinning Applications to the Start Menu

To pin an app to the Start menu, follow these steps:
1. Click on the Start button in the taskbar.
2. Locate the app you wish to pin either in the list or by using the search box to search for its name.
3. Press and hold (or right-click) the app.
4. From the context menu that appears, choose 'Pin to Start.'

To remove an app from the Start menu, simply select 'Unpin from Start.'

Changing the Date and Time

If you wish to modify the date and time settings in Windows 11, you have two approaches: automatic and manual adjustment. Here are the steps for both methods:

Automatic Time Setting:

1. Open Settings by clicking on the Start icon, followed by the gear icon.
2. In the sidebar, select 'Time & Language,' and then 'Date & Time' on the right.

3. Enable the switch next to 'Set time automatically,' and ensure your time zone is correctly detected. If desired, you can also enable the switch for 'Adjust for daylight saving time automatically' if you want Windows 11 to handle this for you.

Manual Time Setting:

1. Open Settings and navigate to 'Time & Language' > 'Date & Time' as previously described.
2. Disable the switch next to 'Set time automatically.'
3. Click 'Change' under 'Set the date and time manually.' A window will appear, allowing you to select your preferred date and time. Confirm your choices by clicking 'Change.'
4. If needed, you can also manually adjust your time zone by using the drop-down menu under 'Time Zone.

Changing the Time in Windows Control Panel on Windows 11

1. Click on the Search icon (the magnifying glass) located on the Windows 11 taskbar.
2. Type Control Panel in the search bar and click on the Control Panel app in the search results to open it.
3. Within the Control Panel, click on Clock and Region.
4. Next, select Date and Time.
5. To adjust the time and date manually, click on the appropriate settings.
6. Finally, confirm your changes by selecting OK.

Cortana

Cortana is Microsoft's personal productivity assistant that helps you save time and focus attention on what matters most. It offers users a swift means of accessing information within Microsoft 365. It facilitates interactions through typed or spoken queries, enabling users to connect with contacts, review calendars, set reminders, create tasks, and perform various other functions efficiently.

Installing Cortana in Windows 11 and Activation

Cortana comes pre-installed but requires activation. Follow these steps to enable and use Cortana:

1. Cortana is pre-installed but isn't active by default. You need to initiate and sign in to the Cortana app to use it.
2. To find Cortana, conduct a Windows Search for Cortana.
3. Alternatively, you can access Cortana by clicking the Windows Start button, selecting All Apps, and then opening the Cortana app.

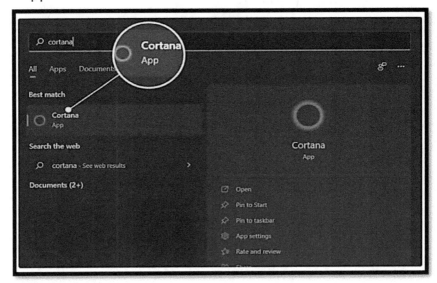

4. The Cortana app will open and display a sign-in prompt. Select Sign In and enter your credentials.

5. A screen will appear to warn you Cortana needs access to personal information to function. Select **Accept and Continue**.

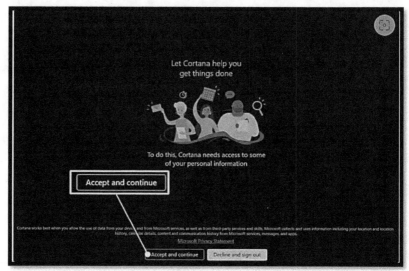

6. The Cortana app will launch. You can now activate Cortana using the Hey Cortana phrase or by entering text into the Cortana app.

NB: Be sure Cortana is also enabled in the **Voice activation** area of **Settings** so that Cortana will wake up when you speak.

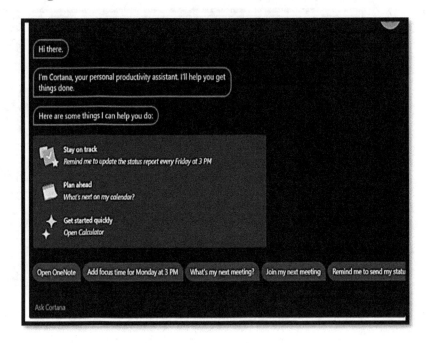

Windows Desktop

Windows Desktop is the main user interface of the Windows operating system. It allows you to access your files, folders, apps, and settings. You can customize your desktop to suit your preferences and needs by changing your desktop background, display settings, themes, colors, and sounds.

Changing your Desktop Background

To personalize the image or color displayed on your desktop background, follow these steps:
1. Click on the Start menu.
2. Select Settings.

3. Navigate to Personalization.
4. Click on Background.
5. Here, you can choose from a variety of options, including a list of preloaded pictures, and solid colors, or even create a dynamic slideshow of images.
6. If you're looking for more themes, you can explore additional options in the Microsoft Store.
7. To use your photos as wallpapers, simply browse and select your desired images.

Changing your Display Settings

To customize various aspects of your display, such as text and app size, screen resolution, color calibration, and orientation, follow these steps:

1. Click the Start button.
2. Select Settings.
3. Go to System.
4. Click on Display.
5. In this menu, you can modify text and app sizes, adjust the screen resolution, calibrate colors, and change the display orientation.
6. Additionally, you can fine-tune the brightness of your screen and configure settings for multiple displays if you have more than one monitor connected to your PC.

Changing Themes, Colors, and sounds

Themes encompass a blend of desktop backgrounds, window colors, and sounds that impart a unique style to your PC.

Themes and colors

To modify the theme and color settings follow these steps:
1. Click on the Start button.
2. Select Settings.
3. Go to Personalization.
4. Click on Colors.
5. In the Choose your color section, choose Custom.
6. Under Choose your default Windows mode, select Dark.
7. Under Choose your default app mode, you can select either Light or Dark based on your preference.

Sounds

To customize the sound scheme for various events on your PC, like receiving new email notifications or encountering error messages, follow these steps:
1. Click the Start button.
2. Select Settings.
3. Navigate to System.
4. Click on Sound.
5. To access the Sound Control Panel, click Sound once more.
6. In the Sound Control Panel, you can configure the sounds associated with different events.

Screen savers

Screen savers are programs that display animations or images on the screen when the computer is idle for a certain period. They were originally designed to prevent burn-in or ghosting on CRT monitors, but they are mostly obsolete in the modern era of LCD monitors.

However, some people still use screen savers for aesthetic or security reasons, or to display personal photos or messages.

While Windows 11 continues to support screen savers, they are no longer enabled by default. You have the option to choose from six built-in screen savers or install additional ones from third-party sources. Furthermore, you can customize the settings for each screen saver, adjusting parameters like duration, speed, color, and text. To activate and configure screen savers in Windows 11, you'll need to access the Screen Saver Settings, which are somewhat concealed within the Settings app. To find it, simply search for screen saver in either the Start menu or the Settings app.

Windows power settings

Windows power settings are options that allow you to control how your computer uses energy and battery. You can adjust various power settings to optimize your PC for performance, battery life, or power saving. One of the power settings you can use is hibernate mode.

Hibernate Mode

Hibernate mode represents a power-saving state wherein your computer conserves energy while retaining your active work. During hibernation, your PC meticulously stores the present system state, encompassing open programs and files, within a dedicated file on your hard drive. Subsequently, it completely powers down, consuming no electrical energy. When you power on your computer once more, it seamlessly resumes operations from where you left off, ensuring the preservation of all data without any loss.

Hibernate mode and sleep mode both serve to preserve your work while transitioning your PC into a low-power state. However, they diverge in how they manage power:

1. Sleep Mode: In sleep mode, your PC conserves power but maintains a minimal level of energy to facilitate faster wake-up times. It's ideal for situations where you need to quickly resume your work.

2. Hibernate Mode: On the other hand, hibernate mode uses no power at all, fully shutting down your computer. While it offers energy savings, it takes a longer time to resume operations. Hibernate mode is advantageous when you want to extend battery life or keep your PC running for extended periods, such as overnight or during extended travel.

Enabling Hibernate Mode in Windows 11:

To utilize hibernate mode, you must first enable it by following these steps:

- Open the Settings menu.
- Click on System.
- On the right side, select Power & battery (or simply Power).
- In the Power section, click on Screen and Sleep to access the settings.
- Scroll to the bottom and click on Additional power settings.
- On the left side, click on Choose what the power buttons do.
- At the top, click on Change settings that are currently unavailable.
- Under Shutdown settings, check the box next to Hibernate.
- Click Save Changes.

Now, you can hibernate your PC by either selecting Start > Power > Hibernate or by configuring your power button or lid-closing options within the same window.

Windows control panel

Windows Control Panel is a feature that allows you to adjust various settings and options for your Windows operating system. It has been around since the first version of Windows, but it is not very prominent in Windows 11.

Accessing the Control Panel in Windows 11:

There are multiple methods to open the Control Panel in Windows 11:

1. **Using the Start Menu:**
   - Click the Start Icon in your taskbar.
   - Type control panel.
   - Click on the Control Panel icon that appears in the search results.

2. Using the Run Menu or Command Prompt:

- Press Windows+R on your keyboard to open the Run window.
- Type control and then click OK or press Enter.
- Alternatively, you can open the Control Panel from the Command Prompt or Windows Terminal by typing control and pressing Enter.

3. Pinning to the Taskbar:

- After opening the Control Panel through any of the methods above, its icon will appear in your taskbar.
- To keep it there for easy access, right-click the Control Panel icon and select Pin to Taskbar.

4. Adding a Desktop Icon:

- Open Settings by pressing Windows+i.
- Navigate to Personalization > Themes.
- Click on Desktop Icon Settings.

- Checkmark Control Panel in the Desktop Icon Settings window and click OK. The Control Panel icon will be added to your desktop.

The Control Panel houses various applets or small programs for configuring different system aspects, such as display, sound, network, and security. You can also directly open specific Control Panel applets through the command center by typing the corresponding Control Panel command line command. For example, entering control appwiz.cpl into the Command Prompt will open the Uninstall or Change a Program applet without the need to access the Control Panel first.

How to Customize the Lock Screen

The lock screen is the first thing you see when you turn on your PC. It shows the date and time, some app notifications, and a background image. You can customize the lock screen to make it more personal and useful.

Customizing Your Lock Screen:

To personalize your lock screen, consider these methods:

1. Changing the Background Image: You have three choices for your lock screen background: Windows Spotlight, Picture, or Slideshow. Windows Spotlight fetches and displays captivating images from Microsoft. With Picture, you can pick a single image from your PC or use default ones. Slideshow lets you select a folder of images to cycle through randomly. To modify your lock screen background, follow these steps:

- Go to Settings > Personalization > Lock screen.

- Under Personalize your lock screen, choose one of the options from the drop-down menu. If you select Picture or Slideshow, you can also add your images by clicking Browse photos or Browse, respectively.

Disabling Lock Screen Tips and Fun Facts

To eliminate the appearance of tips and fun facts on your lock screen, simply uncheck the box labeled Get fun facts, tips, tricks, and more on your lock screen. This adjustment will create a more streamlined lock screen experience.

CONCLUSION

Configuring and customizing offers users the opportunity to put their computing experience to their specific needs and preferences. It provides a robust set of customization options, allowing users to personalize everything from the desktop background to the taskbar layout, and even the behavior of the Start Menu.

Through the Settings app, users can fine-tune system settings, security preferences, and privacy options, ensuring that the operating system aligns with their requirements. This level of control empowers individuals to create a computing environment that suits their workflow, aesthetic preferences, and security considerations.

Furthermore, It offers users a wide range of accessibility features, making it inclusive and accommodating for individuals with diverse needs. These accessibility options, combined with customization features, enable a more user-friendly and personalized computing experience for all.

Cortana in Windows 11 represents a continued evolution of Microsoft's virtual assistant technology. While it has been a prominent feature in previous Windows versions, its role and capabilities have evolved to align better with the changing needs and preferences of users. It has transitioned from a standalone digital assistant to a more integrated and streamlined feature. It now primarily serves as a voice-based productivity tool, offering quick access to information, settings, and actions through voice commands and text queries. This makes it a valuable tool for multitasking and hands-free interactions, especially for users who prefer voice-based input.

While configuring and customizing Windows 11 can be a highly satisfying and empowering process, it's important to remember that changes should be made thoughtfully and with an understanding of the potential impacts on system stability and performance. Regular backups and system restore points are advisable to mitigate any potential issues.

CHAPTER THREE

USER ACCOUNT

User Account Types

In Windows 11, user account types categorize users into different access and privilege levels within the computer system. There are primarily two types of user accounts: Administrator and Standard User. **An Administrator account** grants full control over the device. This means that users with this account type can install applications, execute elevated commands, modify global system configurations, and perform various other actions. Administrator accounts are typically utilized for initial computer setup and the management of other user accounts.

On the other hand, a **Standard User account** imposes limitations on the user, but it provides a highly secure environment. Users with a standard account can launch applications but cannot install new ones. If an application necessitates elevated permissions, the user will receive a prompt to authenticate the action using administrator credentials. Additionally, a standard user account can modify settings, but these changes will only affect their account. It is advisable that all users, including administrators, employ a standard account type for their day-to-day computing tasks.

Creating User Accounts

Setting up user accounts enables you to share your computer with others while safeguarding your files and preferences. The type of account you choose to create determines the level of access and privileges granted to the device. Windows 11 offers two primary types of user accounts: Microsoft accounts and local accounts.

A Microsoft account is an online credential that facilitates sign-in to Windows 11 and provides access to a range of Microsoft services such as OneDrive, Outlook, Xbox, and more. It also allows for the synchronization of your settings, preferences, and files across various devices. To add a Microsoft account you will need an email address or a phone number associated with your account.

 A local account is an offline account limited to the device on which it's created. It doesn't necessitate an email address or phone number, and it doesn't sync with online services. A local account can be advantageous for those seeking enhanced privacy or in cases where an internet connection is unavailable. To create a local account on Windows 11, you simply select a username and set a password.

Creating local account

1. Open the Settings app
2. Click on Accounts.
3. Navigate to the Other Users tab.
4. Under the Other Users section, click the Add Account button.

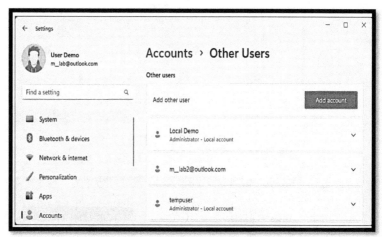

5. Choose the I don't have this person's sign-in information option.

6. Select the Add a user without a Microsoft account option.

7. Provide a name and password for the new local account.

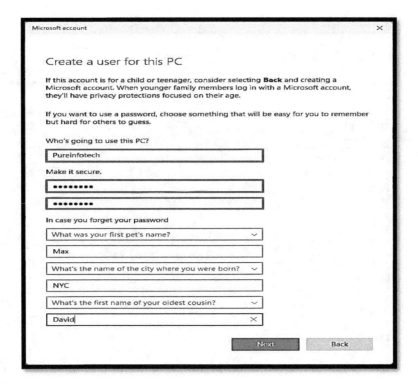

8. Configure security questions to recover the account in case the password is lost.

9. Click the Next button.

10. (Optional) To change the account type, select the newly created account and click the Change account type button.

11. In the Account type drop-down menu, choose the Administrator option if needed.

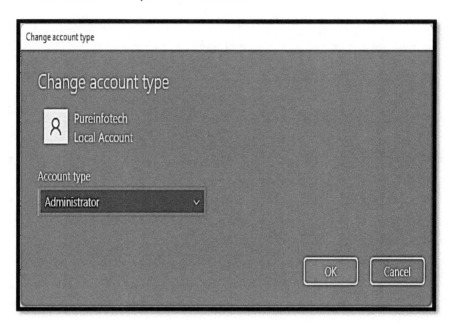

12. Click the OK button.

Is it necessary to establish a Microsoft account for Windows 11?

To run a Microsoft account is typically required by default. While Microsoft accounts are free to create, there are compelling reasons to choose a local account when installing Windows 11, even if it's an option.

Changing Passwords

Changing passwords on Windows 11 is a crucial step in safeguarding your account and device against unauthorized access. The process for changing your password varies depending on the type of account you have. Here are the methods to change your password:

For Microsoft Account Users:

1. On the sign-in screen, input your Microsoft account name (if it's not already displayed). If multiple accounts are present on the computer, select the one you wish to modify.
2. Beneath the password field, choose I forgot my password.
3. Follow the steps to reset your password, which typically involves verifying your identity with a security code sent to your email or phone number.
4. After successfully resetting your password, you can use it to log in to Windows 11 and other Microsoft services.

For Local Account Users:

1. Open the Settings app and go to the Accounts page. The quickest way to access this page is to use the Start menu, search for Password, and select Change your password.
2. Click on Password. Note that this option will only be available if you haven't enabled any Windows Hello authentication tools; otherwise, the Password section won't be displayed.
3. Click Change. A drop-down menu will appear, indicating that you are all set up and offering a Change button that leads to the password setup screens.
4. Enter your current password.
5. Provide your new password along with a hint. Unlike some other operating systems, Windows 11 requires a hint entry, so be sure to enter something. Choosing an obscure hint or one that is deliberately misleading can enhance password security.
6. Click Finish to confirm the password change.

If you have a Local Account and Forgot Your Password:

1. After entering an incorrect password, select the Reset password link on the sign-in screen. If you use a PIN instead, refer to PIN

sign-in issues. Note that if you're using a work device connected to a network, the option to reset your password or PIN may not be available, in which case, contact your administrator.

2. Answer your security questions.
3. Set a new password.
4. Sign in as usual using the new password.

Switching Users

Switching user accounts allows you to share your computer with others while safeguarding your files and settings. Depending on your account type, you can have varying levels of access and privileges on the device. Windows 11 offers several methods for switching user accounts, each with its convenience. Here are brief steps for each method:

Using the Start menu:
1. Click the Windows icon in the taskbar.
2. Click your profile image.
3. Select the desired user account from the context menu.
4. Enter the password for that account to switch.

Using Ctrl+Alt+Delete:
1. Simultaneously press Ctrl+Alt+Delete on your keyboard.
2. Choose Switch User on the screen that appears.
3. You'll be directed to the login screen, where you can select the user account to switch to.

Using Alt+F4:
1. While on the desktop, press Alt+F4 on your keyboard.
2. Click the down arrow next to the text box.
3. Select Switch User from the drop-down menu.
4. Click OK or press Enter on your keyboard.
5. Proceed to the login screen to select a different user account.

Using Windows Terminal (Windows 11 Pro or higher):
1. Right-click the Windows icon in the taskbar and select Windows Terminal (Admin) to open Windows Terminal with administrator privileges.
2. Run the command: **tsdiscon**.
3. Your screen will lock.
4. Unlock the screen, and you'll arrive at the login screen, where you can choose the user account to switch to.

NB: the Windows Terminal method is exclusive to Windows 11 Pro or higher editions.

Creating a password Reset Disk

Creating a password reset disk is a proactive measure to regain access to your local account if you ever forget your password. This disk, typically a USB flash drive, contains a file that can unlock your account. It's essential to create this reset disk before you forget your password, as doing so afterward won't be possible. Here are the steps to create a password reset disk:

1. Insert an empty USB flash drive into your computer.
2. Click the Search button located in the middle of the taskbar and type the password reset disk into the search box at the top.
3. When the Create a password reset disk option appears in the search results, click on it to open the utility.

4. The Forgotten Password Wizard will launch. Click Next to proceed.
5. From the drop-down menu, select the USB flash drive you inserted earlier and then click Next.
6. Enter your current local account password and click Next.
7. Allow the wizard to create the password reset disk. Once it's finished, click Next and then Finish.

You have now successfully generated a password reset disk for your local account. Make sure to store it in a secure place and use it exclusively when you need to reset your password.

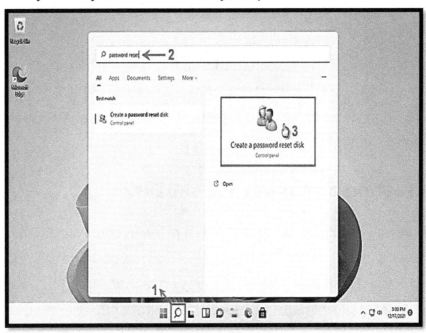

CONCLUSION

User accounts play a fundamental role in shaping the computing experience and ensuring the security and privacy of users. These accounts provide a framework for managing individual access to the operating system, applications, and files, allowing for customization and personalization while maintaining system integrity.

Windows 11 offers a variety of user account types, including local accounts and Microsoft accounts, each with its own set of features and benefits. Microsoft accounts, in particular, provide seamless integration with various Microsoft services, such as OneDrive and the Microsoft Store, enhancing cross-device synchronization and productivity.

CHAPTER FOUR

INSTALLING DEVICES

Installing Printers / Scanners

Installing printers or scanners is a multi-step process that involves connecting the device to your computer or network and configuring it through the Settings app or other methods. Depending on the type of printer or scanner you have, you may need to install additional drivers or software to ensure proper functionality. Here are the general steps to install printers or scanners:

1. For USB Printers or Scanners:

- Plug your USB printer or scanner into your computer.
- Turn on the device.
- Windows 11 should automatically detect it and install the necessary drivers.
- Confirm that the device is ready to use by navigating to Settings > Bluetooth & devices > Printers & scanners.

2. For Wireless Printers or Scanners:

- Ensure that your wireless printer or scanner is connected to the same network as your computer.
- Refer to the device's manual or website for instructions on connecting it to your Wi-Fi network.
- Go to Settings > Bluetooth & devices > Printers & scanners.
- Click Add Device, and Windows 11 will search for available devices.

- Select your device from the list of options and follow the on-screen instructions to add it.

3. For Older Printers or Scanners Not Detected Automatically:

- If your older printer or scanner isn't automatically detected, you can add it manually using the legacy wizard.
- Go to Settings > Bluetooth & devices > Printers & scanners.
- Click Add device, wait a few seconds, and then select Add manually.
- Choose My printer is a little older and follow the wizard's steps to locate and install the device.

4. For Network Printers or Scanners Using TCP/IP:

- To add a network printer or scanner with a TCP/IP connection, follow these steps:
- Go to Settings > Bluetooth & devices > Printers & scanners.
- Click Add device, wait briefly, and then choose Add manually.
- Select Add a printer using a TCP/IP address or hostname.
- Follow the wizard's instructions to enter the device's IP address or hostname, port name, and driver.

5. For Local Printers or Scanners with Non-USB Ports (e.g., LPT1 or COM1):

- If you have a local printer or scanner using a different port than USB, follow these steps:
- Go to Settings > Bluetooth & devices > Printers & scanners.
- Click Add device, wait for a moment, and then select Add manually.
- Choose Add a local printer or network printer with manual settings.
- Follow the wizard's prompts to select the port, driver, and printer name.

How to Automatically Add a Printer

Adding a printer is a process when Windows that can automatically identify the device. You can accomplish this in just a couple of minutes with minimal user intervention. Here's how:

1. Open Settings: You can access Settings in several ways. One option is to right-click the Start button and choose Settings. Alternatively, you can use the keyboard shortcut WIN+i.

2. Navigate to Printers & Scanners: Inside the Settings app, go to Bluetooth & devices, and then select Printers & scanners.

3. Select Add Device: Click the Add Device option. Give Windows a few seconds to search for available printers.

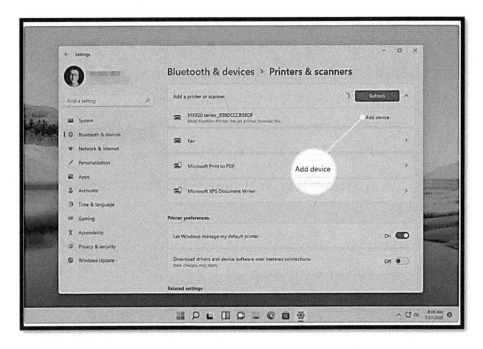

4. Choose the Printer: Once Windows identifies the printer, click Add Device next to the one you want to install.

5. Wait for Installation: Allow Windows to complete the installation process. The newly added printer will now be visible in the list alongside any other printers and scanners you already use.

NB: For Older Printers: If you have an older printer that doesn't appear in the list, choose Add manually instead. Then, select My printer is a little older and click Help me find it to initiate a search. If you need assistance adding a printer not listed, refer to the manual instructions below.

How to Manually Add a Printer

If your computer doesn't automatically recognize the printer, you can add it manually with these steps:

1. **Open Settings**: Go to Settings and then navigate to Bluetooth & devices > Printers & scanners > Add device.

2. **Wait for Detection**: Give Windows a few moments to try and locate the printer automatically. When you see the Add manually link, select it.

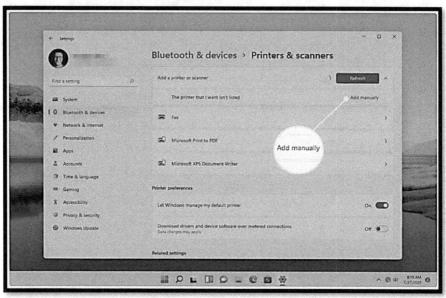

3. **Choose Connection Method**: Depending on your printer's connection method, you have several options. All five options work for wireless or network-attached printers. If your printer is directly connected to your computer, choose Add a local printer or network printer with manual settings, and then click Next.

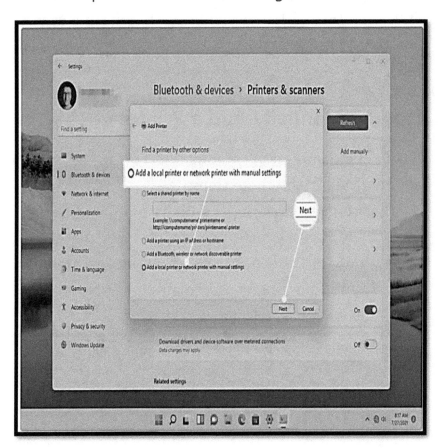

4. **Select the Port**: Choose the port your printer is connected to, and then select Next. If it's connected via USB, you can find it in the list. There are also options for parallel (LPT) and serial (COM) ports.

5. **Install the Printer Driver**: Next, you'll need to install the printer driver. If the printer comes with a driver disc, select Have Disk to browse for it. Otherwise, choose Windows Update. Windows will take a moment to update the list of available printers.

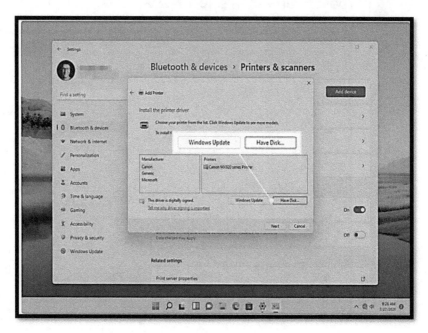

6. **Choose the Printer Model**: Select the manufacturer from the left column and then the model from the right column. Click Next.

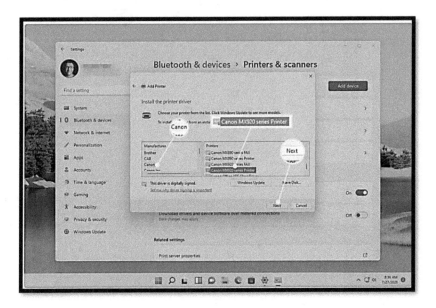

7. **Name the Printer**: Give your printer a name (for reference purposes), and then select Next.

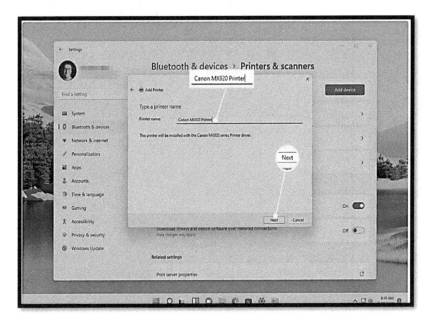

8. **Driver Version**: If prompted to choose a driver version, select Replace the current driver unless you're sure the installed driver is correct, in which case, choose Use the driver that is currently installed.

9. **Printer Installation**: Wait while Windows installs the printer driver.

10. **Printer Sharing**: Choose Do not share this printer unless you want to share it with other devices on your network, in which case, select Share this printer and provide the necessary details.

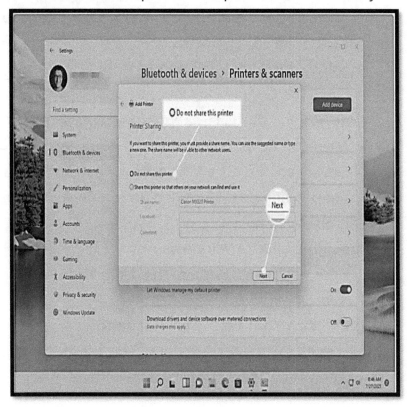

11. **Success**: You'll see a success page. You can choose to print a test page to check the printer's functionality, or simply click Finish to see the printer listed in your devices.

Connecting a smartphone to your computer

Linking an Android phone to a Windows 11 PC is a seamless process that enhances the integration between your smartphone and your PC. By connecting the two devices, you can enjoy several convenient features and functionalities. Here's a more detailed guide on how to achieve this:

1. Ensure You Meet Requirements:
- To link your Android phone to Windows 11, you'll need a Microsoft account. If you don't have one, you can create it during the setup process.

2. Download the Link to Windows App:
- Open the Google Play Store on your Android phone.
- Search for the Link to Windows app, which is developed by Microsoft Corporation.
- Download and install the app on your Android device. The app may already be preinstalled on certain Android phones, while it is always preinstalled on all Windows 11 PCs.

3. Launch the Link to Windows App:
- After installation, open the Link to Windows app on your Android phone.

4. Sign In with Your Microsoft Account:
- In the Link to Windows app, you will be prompted to sign in with your Microsoft account credentials.

- Enter your email address and password associated with your Microsoft account.

5. Grant Permissions:
- The app will request various permissions to establish a connection between your Android device and Windows 11.

Grant these permissions to enable the full functionality of the linking process.

6. Connect Your Android Phone to Windows 11:

- On your Windows 11 PC, navigate to the Windows Settings (you can access this by clicking the Start button and then selecting the gear icon).
- In Settings, click on Phone or Phone Calls (depending on your Windows 11 version).
- Under the Link your Android phone section, click on Add a phone.
- Follow the on-screen instructions to complete the setup process, which may include verifying your identity through your Android phone.

7. Configure Sync and Features (Optional):

- Once linked, you can configure various synchronization settings between your Android phone and Windows 11, such as message and notification syncing. You can also access features like screen mirroring and more, depending on your device and software capabilities.

8. Enjoy Cross-Device Functionality:

- Once the setup is complete, your Android phone will be linked to your Windows 11 PC. You can now enjoy the benefits of seamless integration, including the ability to access your phone's notifications, messages, photos, and more directly from your PC.

By following these steps, you can establish a secure and convenient connection between your Android phone and Windows 11, allowing for a more integrated and efficient computing experience across both devices.

Mouse Settings

Mouse Settings is a feature that allows you to customize various aspects of your mouse, such as the pointer speed, size, color, style, and buttons. You can also enable Mouse Keys, which lets you use the numeric keypad to move the mouse pointer and perform clicks.

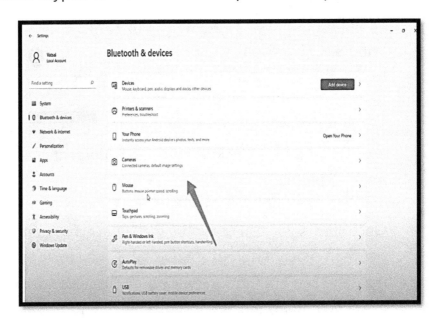

Setting the mouse for Left-handed people

Configuring the primary mouse button is a simple but essential customization that allows users to define which mouse button (left or right) performs the primary (default) click action. This customization can be particularly useful for left-handed users or those who prefer an alternative mouse button configuration. Here's a detailed guide on how to set the primary mouse button:

1. Open the Start Menu:

- Click on the Start button, typically located at the bottom left corner of the desktop.

2. Access the Settings App:

- Click on the gear-shaped Settings icon in the Start menu.

3. Navigate to Bluetooth & Devices:

- Within the Settings app, locate and click on Bluetooth & devices. This section allows you to manage various devices and peripherals, including your mouse.

4. Select the Mouse Option:

- Under the Bluetooth & devices section, find and click on the Mouse option. This opens the mouse settings where you can customize your mouse behavior.

5. Adjust the Primary Mouse Button:

- In the Mouse settings, look for the Primary mouse button drop-down menu. Click on this drop-down menu to reveal your options.

6. Choose Left or Right as the Primary Mouse Button:

- In the drop-down menu, you will see two choices: Left and Right. Select the option that corresponds to your preferred primary mouse button configuration.
- **Left**: This option makes the left mouse button the primary button, which is the default setting for most users.
- **Right**: Choosing this option designates the right mouse button as the primary button, which can be useful for left-handed users or those who prefer this configuration.

7. Apply the Changes:

- After selecting your preferred primary mouse button, the changes are typically applied automatically. You can confirm this adjustment by using your mouse, and the selected button will now act as the primary button for click actions.

8. Test Your Mouse Configuration:

- To ensure that the new primary button setting suits your needs, try using your mouse for various tasks, such as opening files, selecting items, and interacting with applications.

Changing the color of the Mouse cursor on Windows 11

Customizing the appearance of your mouse pointer can make it more visible and easier to locate on your screen. This is particularly helpful for users with visual impairments or those who simply prefer a more distinct and personalized mouse pointer. Here's a detailed guide on how to change the color and size of the mouse pointer:

1. Open the Start Menu:
- Click on the Start button, usually located at the bottom left corner.

2. Access the Settings App:
- Click on the gear-shaped Settings icon within the Start menu.

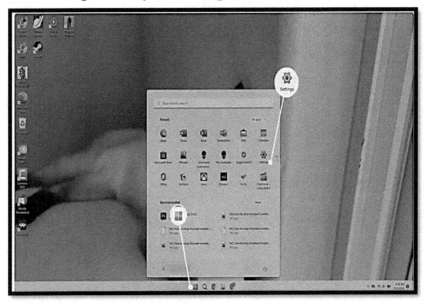

3. Navigate to Accessibility Settings:

- Inside the Settings app, look for and click on Accessibility in the left sidebar. This section contains various accessibility-related options.

4. Customize Mouse Pointer:

- Under the Accessibility settings, find and select Mouse pointer and touch under the Vision category.

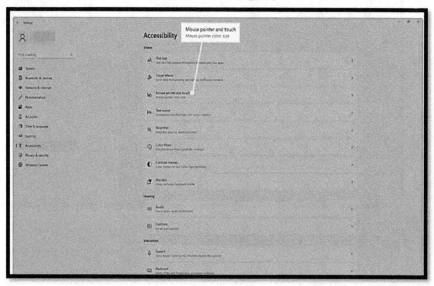

5. Customize Mouse Pointer Settings:

- In the Cursor & pointer settings, you'll find various options to tailor the appearance of your mouse pointer to your preferences. Here's how to customize your mouse pointer:

- **Change Mouse Pointer Color**: Under the Mouse Pointer section, click on the Color drop-down menu. You can choose from various colors to change the color of your mouse pointer. Select the color that provides the best visibility for your needs.

- **Adjust Mouse Pointer Size**: In the same Cursor & pointer settings, you'll find the Size slider. Move the slider to the right to increase the size of your mouse pointer or to the left to make it smaller. This allows you to choose a pointer size that suits your comfort and visibility requirements.

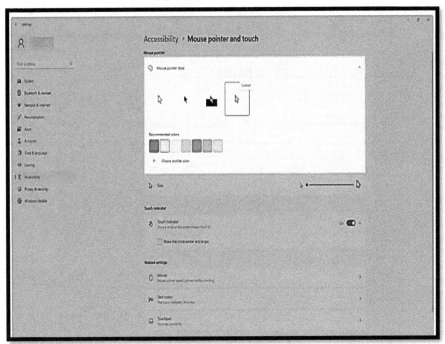

6. Apply Your Customizations:

- After selecting your preferred mouse pointer color and size, your changes should take effect immediately. You can confirm the adjustments by moving your mouse pointer around the screen.

7. Fine-Tune Additional Pointer Settings (Optional):
- Windows 11 also offers additional customization options, such as choosing a different pointer shape or enabling pointer trails for enhanced visibility. Explore these options in the same Cursor & pointer settings if you wish to further tailor your mouse pointer to your liking.

8. Test Your Mouse Pointer Configuration:
- Try using your mouse pointer for various tasks to ensure that the color and size settings you've chosen provide a comfortable and visible cursor for your computing needs.

Changing the Mouse pointer size

To modify the appearance of your mouse pointer you have several options for adjusting its size and color. Here are two methods to customize your mouse pointer:

Method 1: **Using Windows Settings**
1. Click on the Start button, typically located in the bottom left corner of your desktop.
2. Select Settings (a gear-shaped icon) to open the Windows Settings app.
3. In the Settings app, click on Accessibility.
4. In the Accessibility settings, select Mouse pointer and touch.
5. Here, you can adjust the size and color of your mouse pointer to your liking.

Method 2: **Using Control Panel**

1. Open the Control Panel. You can do this by searching for Control Panel in the Windows search bar or by right-clicking the Start button and selecting Control Panel.

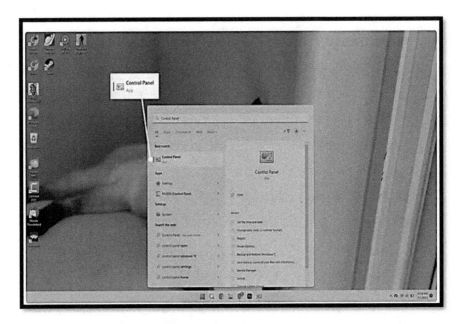

2. In the Control Panel, click on Ease of Access.

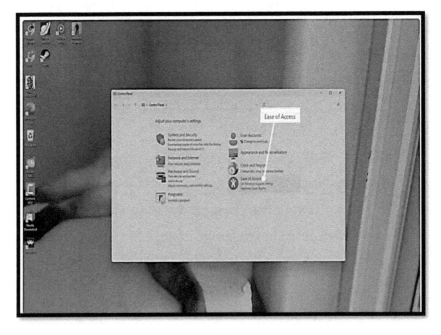

3. Under Ease of Access Center, click on Change how your mouse works.

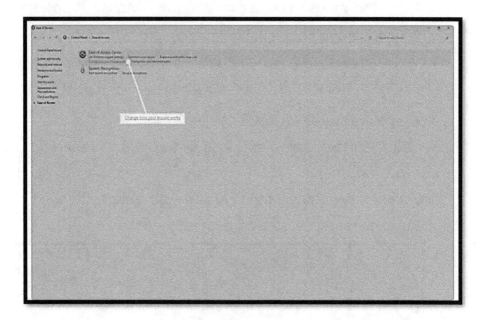

4. Choose Choose a pointer to customize your mouse pointer.

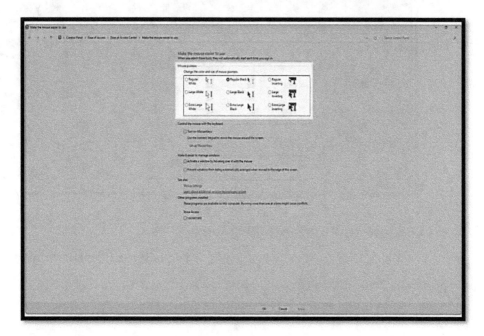

Changing the Mouse cursor scheme

Modifying the mouse pointer in Windows Mouse Properties allows you to select or import a custom scheme for your mouse cursor. You can even change how the cursor appears in various states, enhancing your overall user experience. Here's a step-by-step guide:

1. Access Windows Settings:
- Click on the Start menu icon in the Windows taskbar to open the Start menu.
- Within the Start menu, locate and select the Settings app, usually represented by a gear-shaped icon.

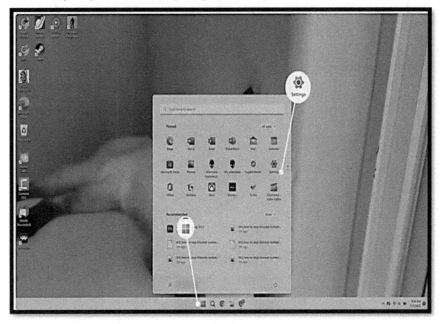

2. Navigate to Bluetooth & Devices:
- Inside the Settings app, find and click on Bluetooth and devices in the left sidebar. This section contains settings related to connected devices.

3. Open Additional Mouse Settings:

- Within the Bluetooth and devices settings, scroll down until you find and select Additional mouse settings.

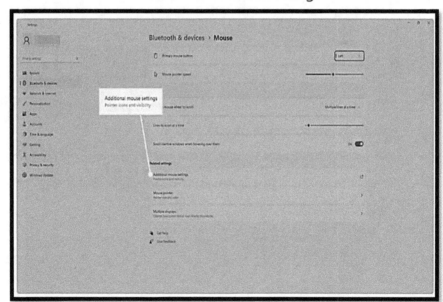

4. Explore Mouse Properties:

- In the Mouse Properties window that appears, click on the Pointers tab. This tab is where you can customize your mouse pointer.

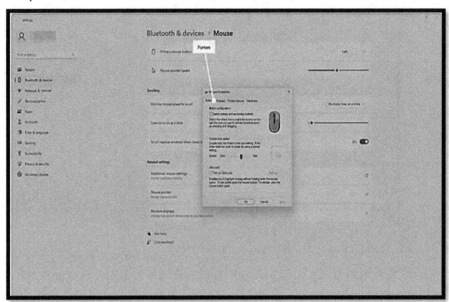

5. Choose a Cursor Scheme:

- Under the Scheme section, click the dropdown menu. Here, you can select a cursor scheme that suits your preferences in terms of size, color, and more. If you've downloaded and installed a custom cursor pack, it will appear in this list.
- Note: When downloading cursor schemes or files from third-party sources, be cautious to avoid potential malware or security risks.

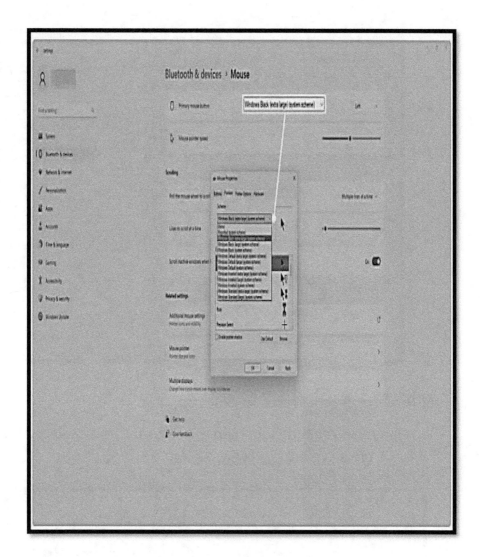

6. Customize Individual Cursor States (Optional):

- Beneath the scheme selection, you have the option to customize individual cursor states within your chosen scheme. To select a custom file for a specific cursor state, click Browse.

NB: Cursor files typically have the file extensions.CUR or.ANI.

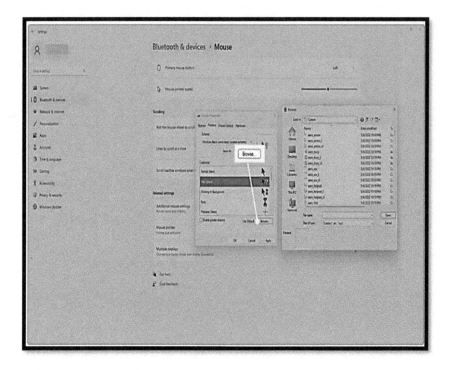

7. Apply Changes:

- Once you've made your cursor customizations, select Apply and
  then OK to save your changes.

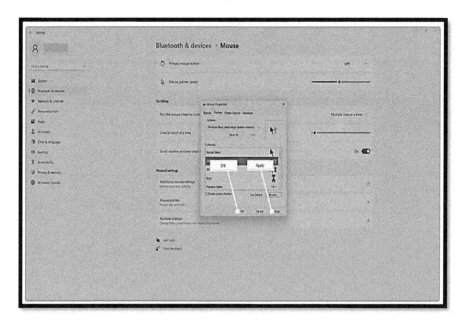

Changing the mouse pointer motion speed on Windows 11

Adjusting the mouse pointer motion speed allows you to control how quickly your cursor moves across the screen as you move your mouse. You can put this speed to match your comfort and precision preferences. Windows 11 offers various methods to change the mouse speed, including the Settings app, Control Panel, and Registry Editor. Here are concise steps for each approach:

Using the Settings App:

Step 1: Open Windows Settings

- Click on the Start button, typically located in the bottom left corner of your desktop.
- Select Settings (a gear-shaped icon) to open the Windows Settings app.

Step 2: Access Bluetooth & Devices

- Inside the Settings app, locate and click on Bluetooth & Devices in the left sidebar. This section contains settings related to connected devices.

Step 3: Choose Mouse Settings

- In the Bluetooth & Devices settings, scroll down until you find and select the Mouse option in the window that opens.

Step 4: Adjust Mouse Pointer Speed

- In the Mouse settings, you'll see a slider next to Mouse Pointer Speed. Use this slider to modify the speed of your mouse pointer to your desired preference. Moving it to the right will increase the speed while moving it to the left will decrease it.

Using Control Panel:

1. Open Control Panel.
2. Go to Hardware and Sound and click on Devices and Printers.

3. Right-click on your mouse device and choose Mouse settings.
4. In the Mouse Properties window, go to the Pointer Options tab.
5. Under Motion, adjust the slider to change the pointer speed.
6. Optionally, enable or disable Enhance pointer precision here.

Using Registry Editor:
1. Launch Registry Editor by pressing the Windows + R keys, typing regedit, and hitting Enter.
2. Navigate to HKEY_CURRENT_USER\Control Panel\Mouse in the Registry Editor.
3. Locate MouseSpeed and double-click it. Modify its value data to 0 (slow), 1 (medium), or 2 (fast).
4. Find MouseThreshold1 and MouseThreshold2 and double-click them to adjust the acceleration of the pointer. Lower values result in faster acceleration.

Making the mouse pointer more evident on Windows 11

If you find it challenging to locate your mouse pointer on the screen, Windows 11 offers several features to make it more visible and easier to track. For instance, you can activate pointer trails, which create a trail of pointers following your cursor's movement. Additionally, you can display your pointer's location by pressing the Ctrl key, which highlights it with a circle. Here are the steps to enable these features:

To Enable Pointer Trails:
1. Open Control Panel.
2. Navigate to Hardware and Sound, and then click on Devices and Printers.
3. Right-click on your mouse device, and select Mouse settings.

4. In the Mouse Properties window, go to the Pointer Options tab.

5. Under Visibility, check the box next to Display pointer trails.

6. Adjust the slider to determine the length of the trails.

7. Click Apply and then OK to save your changes.

To Show the Location of Your Pointer When Pressing Ctrl:

1. Open Settings.

2. Go to Accessibility and select Mouse pointer and touch.

3. Under Pointer options, enable the toggle switch next to Show location of pointer when I press the Ctrl key.

4. Now, whenever you press the Ctrl key, your cursor will be encircled by a visible highlight.

Enabling the mouse keys on Windows 11

You can conveniently toggle the Mouse Keys feature on or off in Windows using a simple keyboard shortcut. Here's how to do it:

1. Press the Alt + Left Shift + Num Lock keys.

- This key combination serves as a quick shortcut to enable or disable Mouse Keys on your Windows computer. It allows you to switch between controlling the mouse pointer using the keyboard (Mouse Keys turned on) and returning to regular mouse control (Mouse Keys turned off).

Here's a breakdown of what each key does in this combination:

- **Alt Key (Alt):** This key is often used to access keyboard shortcuts and menu options in various applications. In this case, it acts as part of the shortcut sequence.

- **Left Shift Key (Left Shift):** The Left Shift key is another modifier key used to create keyboard shortcuts. It also plays a role in activating or deactivating Mouse Keys.

- **Num Lock Key (Num Lock):** The Num Lock key toggles the numeric keypad on and off. When combined with Alt and Left Shift, it functions as the trigger to turn Mouse Keys on or off.

By pressing these three keys simultaneously, you can quickly switch between using Mouse Keys and regular mouse control, providing greater accessibility and flexibility when navigating your Windows operating system.

Mouse Keys is a valuable accessibility feature that allows you to utilize your numeric keypad as a substitute for a traditional mouse. This functionality can be particularly handy when you don't have a physical mouse connected to your computer or require an alternative method for navigating and interacting with the mouse pointer. To enable Mouse Keys, you can follow these steps:

1. Open Settings (Win+I): To access the Windows Settings, press the Windows key (Win) and the letter I (for India) simultaneously on your keyboard. Alternatively, you can navigate to the Start menu and click the gear-shaped Settings icon.

2. Access Accessibility Settings:

- Once in the Settings app, locate and click on Accessibility in the sidebar. This section contains various accessibility-related options to enhance your Windows experience.

3. Enable Mouse Keys:

- Scroll down within the Accessibility settings to the Interaction section and click on Mouse.

- In the Mouse settings, turn on the toggle switch located next to Mouse Keys. Enabling this option activates the Mouse Keys functionality.

- You can further tailor your Mouse Keys experience by adjusting the mouse speed and acceleration using the sliders provided below the toggle switch.

With Mouse Keys enabled, you can now use your numeric keypad for various mouse-related tasks:

- The 2, 4, 6, and 8 keys control pointer movement in the four primary directions (up, left, right, and down).
- The 1, 3, 7, and 9 keys allow for diagonal pointer movement.
- The 5 key functions as a left-click.
- The / key functions as a right-click.
- The * key simulates both a left- and right-click simultaneously.
- The 0 key locks a left-click for dragging items.
- The . key releases the left click.

Installing USB Devices

Installing USB devices is a process that involves connecting the device to your computer and letting Windows 11 detect and install the necessary drivers. Depending on the type of USB device you have, you may need to follow different steps or use additional software to make it work properly. Here are some general steps to install USB devices:

1. Plug and Play Devices:

- For USB devices that are compatible with Windows 11, such as mice, keyboards, flash drives, printers, scanners, or webcams, simply plug the device into your computer's USB port.
- Windows 11 will automatically detect the device and initiate the driver installation process.
- You'll see notifications indicating Setting up your device and that Your device is ready to use.

- To view the status of your device, you can go to Settings > Bluetooth & devices > Devices.

2. Devices Requiring Specific Drivers or Software:
- Some USB devices, like gaming controllers, audio interfaces, or external hard drives, may require you to manually download and install their specific drivers or software.
- Visit the manufacturer's website to find and download the required drivers or software for your device.
- Alternatively, you can use Device Manager to update or install the drivers for your device. To access Device Manager, press the Windows + X keys and select Device Manager from the menu.
- Locate your device under the appropriate category, right-click on it, and choose either Update driver or Install driver.

3. Troubleshooting Undetected USB Devices:
- If Windows 11 fails to detect your USB device, especially older or incompatible ones, you may need to troubleshoot the issue.
- Common troubleshooting steps include:
- Checking the USB port and cable for physical damage.
- Restarting your computer to refresh USB connections.
- Enabling USB legacy support in your computer's BIOS settings.
- Disabling fast startup in power settings.
- Uninstalling and reinstalling the device in Device Manager.

These troubleshooting methods can help resolve issues when your USB device is not recognized by Windows 11.

Download a USB driver for Windows 11?

To download a USB driver follow these steps in detail:

1. Access Device Manager:

- First, open the Windows 11 search bar by clicking on the magnifying glass icon in the taskbar or pressing the Windows key + S.
- Type Device Manager into the search bar and hit Enter. You should see Device Manager as one of the search results.

2. Open Device Manager:

- Click on Device Manager in the search results to open the application. This tool allows you to manage and update hardware drivers on your computer.

3. Locate Universal Serial Bus Controllers:

- In the Device Manager window, you will find a list of hardware categories. Look for Universal Serial Bus controllers in the list. This category represents your USB drivers and controllers.

4. Expand the USB Controllers Category:

- To view the USB drivers, click on the arrow or plus sign next to Universal Serial Bus Controllers. This will expand the category and display a list of USB drivers and controllers installed on your system.

5. Select the USB Driver:

- Identify the specific USB driver that you want to update. Right-click on the USB driver you wish to update. A context menu will appear.

6. Update the USB Driver:

- In the context menu, select the Update driver option. This initiates the driver update process.

7. Choose Automatic Update:

- Windows will present you with two options for updating the driver: Search automatically for updated driver software and Browse my computer for driver software.

- Choose the first option, Search automatically for updated driver software. This option allows Windows to search for the latest driver online and install it automatically if found.

8. Follow On-Screen Instructions:
- Windows will now search for an updated USB driver online. If it finds one, it will download and install it automatically.
- Follow any on-screen instructions or prompts to complete the update process. Windows may require you to restart your computer to apply the changes.

Installing USB 3.0 Drivers on Windows 11

By default, Windows 11 usually installs USB 3.0 drivers. However, in cases where USB 3.0 devices aren't functioning correctly, the USB 3.0 drivers may be absent or damaged. In such situations, performing a fresh installation of these drivers can resolve the issue. Here's a guide on how to install USB 3.0 drivers:

1. Access Device Manager:
- Begin by opening the Windows Start menu. You can do this by clicking on the Windows icon in the taskbar or pressing the Windows key on your keyboard.
- Conduct a Windows Search for Device Manager in the search bar located within the Start menu. Device Manager should appear as the first search result. Click on it to open the application.

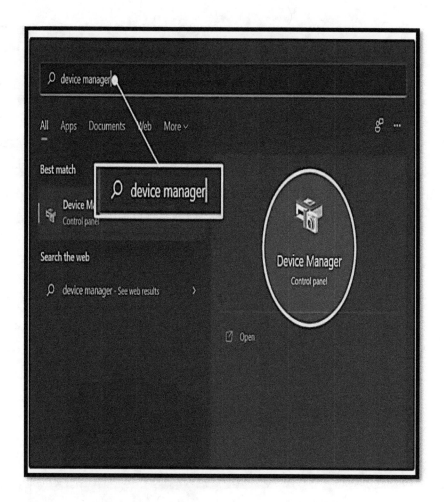

2. Expand the USB Controllers Category:

- In the Device Manager window, you will find a list of hardware categories. Locate the Universal Serial Bus controllers category and click on it to expand the category.

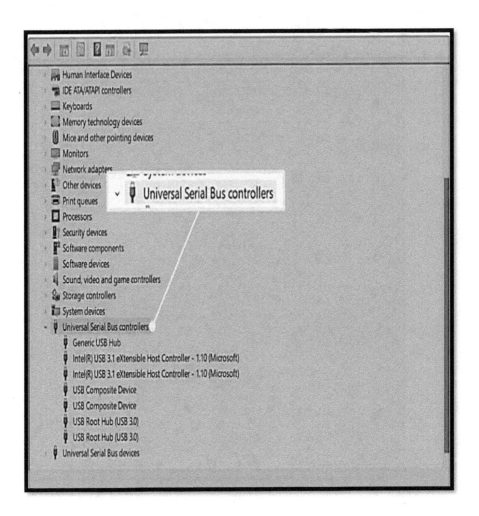

3. Uninstall USB 3.0 Hub (if visible):

- If you can see USB Root Hub (USB 3.0) listed, right-click on it, and from the context menu, select Uninstall device. This step is essential to refresh the USB 3.0 driver.

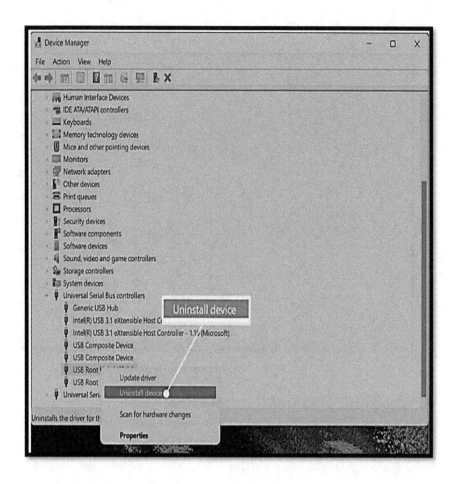

NB: Some PCs may display multiple entries for USB 3.0 hubs. Be sure to uninstall each of them.

4. Scan for Hardware Changes:

- After uninstalling the USB 3.0 hub(s), open the Action menu located at the top of the Device Manager window.
- From the drop-down menu, select Scan for hardware changes. This action prompts Windows 11 to automatically search for new devices, including the USB Root Hub (USB 3.0), and install the necessary drivers.

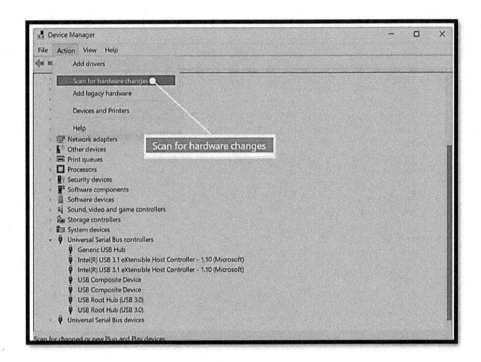

Check for Successful Installation:

- If the installation is successful, you will notice the USB Root Hub (USB 3.0) reappearing in the Device Manager list.

- If, for any reason, the USB Root Hub (USB 3.0) does not reappear, consider rebooting your PC to ensure that the drivers are fully integrated.

Dual Monitor setup

Setting up dual monitors is a great way to improve your productivity and enjoy more screen space. Here are some steps you can follow to set up your multiple monitors:

1. Check Cables and Ports:

- Ensure that you have the appropriate cables (HDMI, DisplayPort, VGA, or DVI) and the compatible ports to connect your monitors to your PC. For desktops with integrated graphics, use the motherboard's ports; for desktops with a dedicated graphics card, use the card's ports.

2. Connect and Power On Monitors:

- Connect your monitors to your PC and power them on. Windows 11 should automatically detect and extend your desktop across them. Alternatively, you can use a wireless display adapter to connect a TV as an additional monitor.

3. Access Display Settings:

- Open the Windows 11 Settings app and click on System, then select Display on the right side of the window. All your connected monitors should be visible in the settings.

4. Identify Monitors:

- To identify which monitor corresponds to which screen, click the Identify button. Numerical labels will briefly appear on each monitor to help you distinguish them.

5. Rearrange Monitors:

- Arrange the monitors on the settings page to match their physical layout. Ensure that they are aligned at the top for seamless mouse movement between screens.

6. Choose Primary Display:

- Select your primary display by clicking on it and scrolling down to the Multiple displays section. Check the box labeled Make this my main display. The primary display will host the Start menu, taskbar, and notification area.

7. Configure Display Mode:

- In the Multiple displays section, choose how you want to use your monitors. Options include extending your desktop, duplicating it, displaying it on one monitor only, or showing it on another monitor.

8. Adjust Display Settings:
- Customize the scale, layout, resolution, orientation, refresh rate, and scaling for each monitor individually in the Scale and Layout section.

9. Access Advanced Display Settings:
- For more advanced settings such as color calibration, HDR mode, night light, and blue light filter, click on Advanced display settings at the bottom of the Display page. You can also access these settings by right-clicking on your desktop and choosing Display settings.

10. Manage Taskbar on Each Monitor:
- To show or hide the taskbar on each monitor, go to Personalization on the left side of Settings, click on Taskbar on the right side, and toggle the switch that says Show taskbar on all displays in the Taskbar behaviors section.

11. Set Background Images:

- Customize the background image for each monitor by clicking Personalization on the left side of Settings, selecting Background on the right side, and choosing a different image for each monitor in the Choose your picture section. Right-click on an image and select Set for monitor 1 or Set for monitor 2 from the context menu.

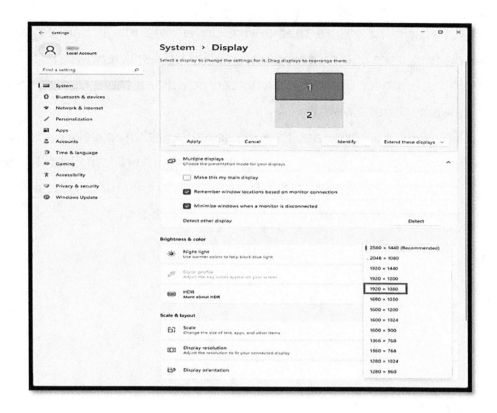

CONCLUSION

The process of installing devices is a vital step in enhancing the functionality and usability of your computer. Whether you're connecting peripherals like printers, scanners, or external drives, or updating drivers for existing hardware components, the way you manage devices directly impacts your overall computing experience.

Windows 11 offers a streamlined and user-friendly approach to device installation. With features like Plug and Play, most devices are automatically recognized and configured upon connection, reducing the need for manual intervention. This simplifies the setup process, making it accessible to users of varying technical expertise.

It's crucial to ensure that device drivers are up-to-date to optimize performance and resolve compatibility issues. Windows Update often includes driver updates, or you can download them directly from the manufacturer's website.

However, it's important to exercise caution during device installation, as improperly installed or incompatible drivers can lead to system instability and errors. Always consult manufacturer documentation and verify driver compatibility before installation.

CHAPTER FIVE

HOW TO INSTALL ANY SOFTWARE

How to install Google Chrome

Google Chrome is a swift and secure web browser that you can easily install on your computer. Here's a step-by-step guide to get Chrome on your system:

1. Access a Web Browser:
- Launch any web browser, such as Microsoft Edge, on your Windows 11 computer.

2. Visit the Google Chrome Download Page:
- Navigate to the official Google Chrome download page by entering the URL or web address for the page.

3. Download Chrome:
- On the Google Chrome download page, locate and click the Download Chrome button.

4. Accept and Begin Download:
- A prompt will appear, presenting Google Chrome's Terms of Service and Privacy Policy. Click the Accept and Install button to initiate the download. Optionally, you can select a different download location if preferred.

5. Save the Installer File:
- Your browser will start downloading a file named ChromeSetup.exe to your computer. After the download is complete, locate this file in your computer's download directory.

6. Run the Installer:

- Double-click on the ChromeSetup.exe file to execute the installer.

7. Permission Confirmation:

- If prompted by the User Account Control (UAC), which asks for permission to make changes to your system, click Yes to authorize the installation process.

8. Installation Progress:

- Wait for the installation to be finalized. Once completed, Google Chrome will launch automatically.

9. Optional Sign-In:

- You have the option to sign in with your Google account to sync your browser settings and bookmarks across devices.

How to make Google Chrome your Default Browser

To set Google Chrome as the default browser in Windows 11, follow these steps:

1. Access Settings:

- Open the Settings app.

2. Navigate to Apps:

- Within the Settings window, click on Apps.

3. Go to Default Apps:

- On the left-hand side of the Apps settings, click on Default apps.

4. Select Google Chrome as Default:

- Locate the Web browser section on the Default apps page.

5. Set Google Chrome as Default:

- Click on the dropdown menu or the option under Web browser and choose Google Chrome to make it the new default browser.

6. Confirm the Change:

- After selecting Google Chrome, click the Set default button to confirm your choice.

7. (Optional) Manage File Associations:
- If you wish to further customize which file types and protocols are associated with Google Chrome, you can click the Choose default apps by file type or Choose default apps by protocol link to make specific adjustments.

8. Save Changes:
- Click the OK button to save your changes and set Google Chrome as your default web browser.

How to Download and Install any Software onto your Windows 11 computer

There are various methods to download and install software on your computer, depending on the source and nature of the software. Here are some general steps to guide you through the process:

1. Downloading from the Internet:
- If you intend to download software from the internet, begin by identifying a trustworthy website that offers the software you require. You can utilize a web browser like Microsoft Edge or Google Chrome to search for the desired software.
- Once the software is downloaded, locate the installer file saved on your computer. Typically, installer files have a .exe extension, signifying that they are executable files capable of installing the software. To initiate the installation, either double-click the installer file or right-click it and select Run as administrator. Follow the on-screen prompts to complete the installation.

2. Installing from a CD-ROM:

- When installing software from a CD-ROM, insert the disc into your computer's CD-ROM drive and allow it to be recognized by your system. Next, open the disc folder and search for the installer file, which is typically named setup.exe or install.exe. Double-click the installer file or right-click it and choose Run as administrator. Follow the on-screen instructions to finalize the installation process.

3. Windows Store Installation:

- To install software from the Windows Store, launch the Store app on your Windows 11 computer and log in using your Microsoft account credentials. Once signed in, you can either browse or search for the desired software. Upon locating it, click on the software's listing, and then click the Get or Install button. The software will be automatically downloaded and installed on your computer.

How to Install VLC Media Player

VLC media player is a versatile, free, and open-source multimedia player capable of handling various media formats, including DVDs, CDs, and streaming protocols. To install a VLC media player on your system, you can follow these steps:

1. Download VLC Media Player:

- Visit the official VLC media player website and click the Download VLC button. If needed, you can select a different version of the setup file that matches your system configuration from the provided drop-down menu.

2. Save and Run the Installer:

- After clicking the download button, you will be prompted to save a file named either vlc-3.0.18-win64.exe (for 64-bit systems) or vlc-3.0.18-win32.exe (for 32-bit systems) to your computer.
- Once the download is complete, locate the downloaded file and double-click it to initiate the installer.

3. Permission Confirmation:

- If User Account Control (UAC) prompts you for permission to make changes to your computer, click Yes to proceed with the installation.

4. Select Language:

- Choose your preferred language for the VLC media player and click OK.

5. License Agreement:

- Click Next to accept the license agreement. You can review the agreement if you wish.

6. Choose Components:

- Select the components you want to install. By default, the VLC media player will install all necessary components for standard functionality. If needed, you can customize the installation by choosing specific components.
- You can also change the destination folder for the installation if desired.

7. Confirm Installation Settings:

- Review your chosen installation settings on the next screen and click Next to proceed.

8. Begin Installation:

- Click Install to start the installation process.

9. Wait for Completion:

- Allow the installation to finish. This may take a few moments.

10. Finish Installation:

- Once the installation is complete, click Finish to exit the installer. You have the option to launch the VLC media player immediately or read the README file for additional information.

To set the VLC media player as your default media player you'll need to adjust some system settings. Follow these steps to make VLC your default player for specific file types:

1. Access Settings:

- Open the Settings app.

2. Navigate to Default Apps:

- Within the Settings window, click on Apps in the left-hand menu.

3. Choose Default Apps by File Type:

- Select Default apps on the right side of the window.

4. Select VLC for File Types:

- Scroll through the list to find the file types you want to associate with the VLC media player, such as .mp4, .mp3, .avi, etc. You can use the search box to locate them quickly.

5. Change Default App:

- Click on the icon of the current default app for each file type, then select VLC media player from the list of available apps.
- Repeat this process for all the file types you want to open with the VLC media player.

How to Install an Antivirus

1. Access the start menu click on the Microsoft Store app and type in Free Antivirus.

2. Type in Free Antivirus and click on Avast free anti-virus and install.

Windows 11 includes a pre-installed antivirus solution known as Microsoft Defender Antivirus, offering continuous protection against malware, viruses, and various threats. It's important to note that, in most cases, there's no necessity to install additional antivirus software on your computer, as Microsoft Defender is proficient at safeguarding your system. However, if you have a preference for an alternative antivirus product, you can install it by following the instructions provided by the software vendor. This typically involves downloading the software from the internet or using a CD-ROM for installation. To ensure smooth operation and prevent conflicts, it's advisable to disable Microsoft Defender Antivirus while running another antivirus program.

To disable Microsoft Defender Antivirus on Windows 11, adhere to these steps:

1. Access Settings:
  - Open the Settings app.

2. Navigate to Privacy & Security:
  - Within the Settings window, click on Privacy & Security in the left-hand menu.

3. Select Windows Security:
  - On the right side of the window, click on Windows Security.

4. Open Windows Security:
  - Click the Open Windows Security button to access the Windows Security application.

5. Access Virus & Threat Protection:
  - In the Windows Security interface, click on Virus & threat protection.

6. Manage Protection Settings:

- Under the Virus & threat protection settings section, click on the Manage settings link.

7. Disable Real-Time Protection:

- Locate the Real-time protection toggle switch and turn it off.

To re-enable Microsoft Defender Antivirus on your system, follow the same steps as above but instead, turn on the Real-time protection toggle switch.

How to Install WhatsApp Messenger

WhatsApp, a widely popular messaging application akin to Telegram, is readily accessible on your mobile device. Additionally, it can be seamlessly utilized on your computer by simply downloading it from the Microsoft Store. In this guide, I will walk you through the process of using WhatsApp and acquiring it through the Microsoft Store.

1. Access the start menu and click on Microsoft Store.

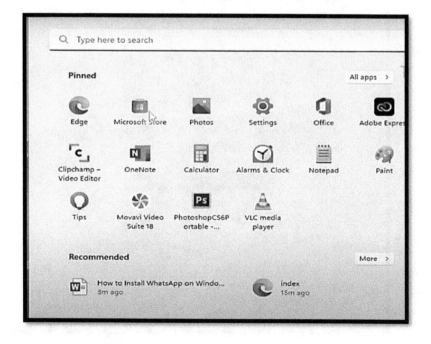

2. On the search bar write WhatsApp an image will pop up for installation.

3. After the installation, click on open to get access to the features.

4. To use WhatsApp on your computer follow the on-screen instructions

How to Zoom Install

To install the Zoom app, please follow these steps:

1. Locate and click on the Microsoft Store icon in your Taskbar.

2. In the Microsoft Store, use the search bar to look for Zoom Cloud Meetings.

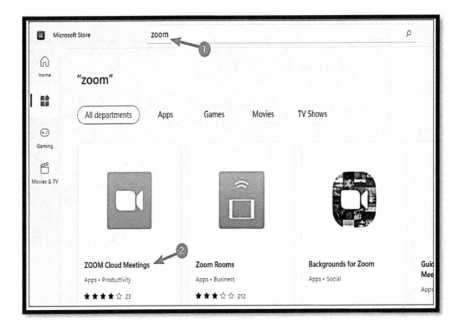

3. Once you've found the Zoom Cloud Meetings app, click on it to view its details.

4. On the app's page, you will see a red Install button. Click on this button.

5. Follow the on-screen instructions provided by the Microsoft Store to complete the installation process.

NB: Ensure you have an internet connection during the installation process, and make sure your system meets the app's requirements for a smooth installation experience.

CONCLUSION

Installing software is a fundamental task that allows users to expand the functionality of their computer and put it to their specific needs. The process has become more streamlined and user-friendly over the years, making it accessible to both beginners and experienced users. Installing software is a process that empowers users to enhance their computing experience. Whether you're downloading apps from the Microsoft Store or installing third-party software, following best practices for security, compatibility, and maintenance is crucial to ensure a smooth and secure computing environment.

CHAPTER SIX

WINDOWS FILE EXPLORER

Windows File Structure

The Windows file structure is the organization and storage system used by the Windows operating system for files and folders. This structure is essential for locating, managing, and safeguarding your data. Windows 11's file structure shares similarities with previous versions like Windows 10 but also brings some differences. Here are key features of the Windows 11 file structure:

1. **C Drive**: The C drive is the default location for the operating system and most applications. It houses system files and settings. Typically, the C drive utilizes a Solid State Drive (SSD), offering faster performance compared to a Hard Disk Drive (HDD).
2. **D Drive**: The D drive is an optional storage location for your files, including documents, pictures, music, videos, and more. Typically, the D drive is an HDD, providing ample storage capacity. Moving personal files to the D drive can free up space on the C drive and enhance system performance.
3. **File Explorer**: File Explorer is the primary tool for accessing and managing files and folders. You can open File Explorer by clicking the folder icon on the taskbar or by pressing Windows + E on your keyboard. In Windows 11, File Explorer features a new design with a simplified toolbar and rounded corners.
4. **Quick Access**: Quick Access in File Explorer displays frequently used or recently accessed files and folders. You can also pin your

favorite items for easy access. Customizing Quick Access is possible by right-clicking it and selecting Options.

5. **OneDrive**: The OneDrive section in File Explorer shows files and folders synced with your Microsoft account and stored in the cloud. OneDrive enables access from any device and facilitates sharing. It also serves as a backup solution for data recovery. You can customize OneDrive settings by right-clicking and choosing Settings.

6. **This PC**: This PC in File Explorer provides an overview of connected drives and devices, such as C drives, D drives, USB flash drives, CD/DVD drives, and more. It also displays storage space and usage information. Right-clicking on drives and devices offers options like Properties, Format, and Eject.

7. **Libraries**: Libraries in File Explorer include default folders for personal files, like Documents, Pictures, Music, and Videos. By default, these folders reside in the C drive under C:\Users\YourName, but you can relocate them to the D drive or elsewhere. You can create custom libraries for specific file types or projects and manage them by right-clicking and selecting options like Properties and Include in the library.

8. **Network**: The Network section in File Explorer presents computers and devices connected to your local network or the internet. It allows file and folder sharing with other users or devices on your network and access to shared resources. You can also stream media content from other devices and access online storage services. Right-clicking on network items provides options like Map network drive, Add a network location, and Connect to a VPN.

Changing file and folder views

There are multiple ways to adjust file and folder views depending on your preferences and requirements. Here are some methods you can utilize:

1. Mouse Scroll Wheel:
- Open the folder for which you want to change the view.
- Press and hold the Ctrl key.
- Use the mouse scroll wheel to cycle through various layout views, including extra-large icons, large icons, medium icons, small icons, lists, details, tiles, or content by scrolling up or down.

2. Keyboard Shortcuts:
- Open the target folder.
- Use keyboard shortcuts to instantly switch to a specific layout view:
- Ctrl + Shift + 1 for extra-large icons.
- Ctrl + Shift + 2 for large icons.
- Ctrl + Shift + 3 for medium icons.
- Ctrl + Shift + 4 for small icons.
- Ctrl + Shift + 5 for list.
- Ctrl + Shift + 6 for details.
- Ctrl + Shift + 7 for tiles.
- Ctrl + Shift + 8 for content.

3. Toolbar Toggle:
- Open the folder you wish to modify the view for.
- Locate the toolbar at the bottom right corner of File Explorer.
- Use the details (left) or large icons (right) button to toggle between details and large icon views.

4. Command Bar:

- Open the folder.
- Access a range of layout views using the command bar at the top of File Explorer.
- Click on the View drop-down button within the command bar.
- Select the desired layout view from the available options.

5. Context Menu:

- Open the folder.
- Right-click on an empty area within the folder's background.
- Over View in the context menu.
- Choose the desired layout view from the list.

6. Applying Folder Views Globally:

- Specify a default template for folders, optimized for General items, Documents, Pictures, Music, or Videos types.
- Open a folder whose view settings you want to apply globally.
- Customize the folder's columns, column width, Group by, Sort by, and layout view settings to your preferences.
- Click the See more (three dots) button in the command bar.
- Select Options.
- Navigate to the View tab.
- Click on the Apply to Folders button.
- Confirm by clicking Yes.
- Click OK to save the changes.

Moving, Copying, Renaming and Deleting Files

Moving, copying, renaming, and deleting files are some of the basic operations that you can perform on your PC. These operations allow you to organize your files and folders according to your preferences and needs.

Moving copying and pasting files and folders

How to Cut, Copy, and Paste Files and Folders Using Drag and Drop
To perform cut, copy, and paste actions for files and folders using drag and drop, follow these steps:
How to Cut, Copy, and Paste Files and Folders in Windows 11 Using Drag and Drop:

1. Open File Explorer and navigate to the file or folder you want to cut or copy. You should be able to see the icon for the item in the right pane of the window.

2. Ensure that the File Explorer window is set to Restore size, not maximized.

3. To open a second File Explorer window, right-click any folder in the Navigation pane or the right pane of the File Explorer window. Select the Open in new window option from the context menu that appears.

4. In the new File Explorer window, navigate to the folder where you want to paste the item you intend to copy or move from the first window.

5. Make sure the second File Explorer window is also set to Restore size and position it next to the first window on your screen.

6. To move an item from the first File Explorer window to the second one, click and hold the file or folder you want to move in the first window. Drag it into the second File Explorer window, and release the mouse button to drop it there.

7. If the files are on the same computer drive, this action will cut and paste or move the item.

8. If the files are on different computer drives, this action will copy and paste the item.

9. Alternatively, to copy the item regardless of the drive they are on, hold down the Ctrl key on your keyboard while dragging and dropping the selected file or folder between the two File Explorer windows.

10. While dragging the item with the Ctrl key held down, you'll see a small plus sign (+) next to your mouse pointer, indicating that the file or folder is being copied instead of cut.

11. Release the mouse button.

12. Finally, release the Ctrl key.

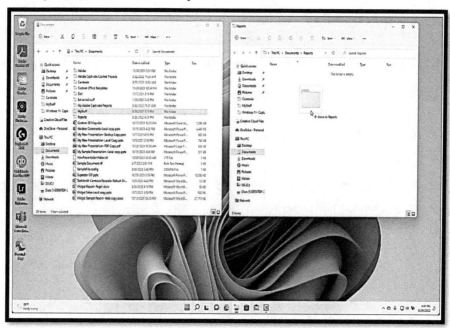

Alternatively, you can utilize keyboard shortcuts to perform cut, copy, and paste actions for files and folders in Windows 11. Here's how:

1. Select the Item:

- In a File Explorer window, first, select the file or folder you intend to copy or move.

2. Copy or Cut:

- To copy the selected item, press the Ctrl + C keys on your keyboard.
- To cut the selected item, press the Ctrl + X keys on your keyboard.

3. Navigate to Destination:
- Use File Explorer to navigate to the folder where you wish to paste the item that you've just copied or cut.

4. Paste:

In the destination folder, press the Ctrl + V keys on your keyboard to paste the copied or cut item into the chosen folder location.

How to Cut, Copy, and Paste Files and Folders Using Ribbon Buttons

- In a File Explorer window, select the file or folder you want to cut or copy.
- Next, click on the desired action, either the Copy or Cut button, located in the Ribbon of the File Explorer window.
- To paste the item you've just cut or copied, navigate to the destination folder using File Explorer. You can choose to use the same File Explorer window if you prefer.
- Once you see the contents of the destination folder displayed in the right pane of the File Explorer window, click on the Paste button in the Ribbon at the top of the File Explorer window to insert the item into the selected folder.

Using File Explorer Toolbar:
- To move a file or folder, select it, navigate to the Home tab in the ribbon at the top of File Explorer, click on Move to, and select the destination from the drop-down menu.

- To copy a file or folder, select it, go to the Home tab in the ribbon, click on Copy to, and choose the destination from the drop-down menu.

Deleting Files and Folder

Deleting files and folders with various methods tailored to your preferences and requirements. Here are several approaches you can choose from:

1. **Using the Delete Key (Recycle Bin):** Simply select the files or folders you wish to remove, and then press the Delete key on your keyboard. If necessary, confirm your action by clicking Yes in a dialog box.
2. **Using Shift + Delete (Permanent Deletion):** To permanently delete selected files and folders without sending them to the Recycle Bin, select the items and press Shift + Delete. You might need to confirm this action by clicking Yes in a dialog box.
3. **Utilizing the Context Menu or Command Bar:** Right-click on the files or folders you want to delete, and then click on the delete icon (depicted as a trash bin) in the context menu. Alternatively, you can locate the delete icon in the command bar at the top of File Explorer. Confirm your action if prompted by clicking Yes in a dialog box.

Renaming Files and Folder

1. Begin by launching File Explorer and locating the file or folder you wish to rename within the File Explorer window.
2. Select the target file or folder by clicking on it.

3. At the top of the File Explorer window, you will find the Rename button within the Ribbon. Click on it.

4. This action will place a subtle border around the name of the selected file or folder, indicating that you are now in renaming mode.

5. Carefully type the desired new name for the file or folder directly into the name box.

6. After entering the new name, you can either click outside the name box anywhere in the window or simply press the Enter key on your keyboard. This will confirm and set the new name for the file or folder.

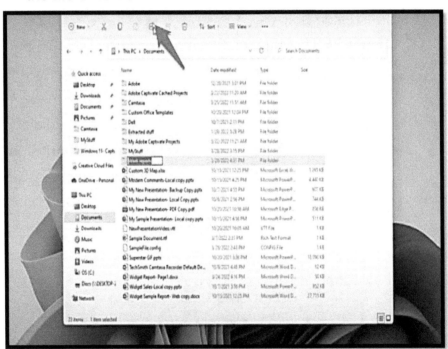

Creating a new folder or Files

Creating a New Folder in File Explorer:

1. Launch File Explorer.

2. Navigate to the desired folder location where you want to create the new folder, whether it's in Documents, Desktop, or elsewhere.

3. Right-click on the chosen location.

4. From the context menu that appears, select New, and then choose the Folder option.

5. Provide a name for the new folder in the highlighted text box.

6. Press the Enter key on your keyboard to confirm and create the new folder.

Default Windows Folders

The default Windows folders refer to folders that the Windows operating system establishes for each user account. These folders serve as designated spaces for storing and managing various file types, including documents, images, music, videos, downloads, and desktop items. Typically, you can find these default Windows folders residing in the C drive under the following path: C:\Users\YourName, with YourName being the name associated with your user account.

The default Windows folders in Windows 11 share similarities with their counterparts in Windows 10, yet exhibit distinctive characteristics in appearance and functionality. Here are key features of the default Windows folders:

1. **Fresh Design Aesthetic:** The default Windows folders in Windows 11 sport a redesigned appearance that harmonizes with the overall visual theme of the operating system. These folders feature rounded corners, vibrant icons, and a simplified toolbar, contributing to a modernized look and feel.

2. **Streamlined Context Menu:** Windows 11 introduces a revamped context menu for default folders, focusing on presenting the most frequently used actions for files and folders. Common operations like open, cut, copy, paste, rename, and delete are prominently displayed. Users also have the option to access the traditional context menu by selecting Show more options or by pressing Shift + F10 on their keyboard.

3. **Command Bar Enhancement:** Instead of the ribbon interface seen in Windows 10, Windows 11 employs a new command bar at the top of File Explorer within default folders. This command bar features three essential buttons: New for creating various file and folder types, See more (represented by three dots) for accessing additional options and settings for File Explorer, and View for adjusting the layout and visual presentation of files and folders.

Searching for Files and Folders

There are various methods to search for files and folders depending on your different needs and preferences. Here are some approaches you can explore:

1. Taskbar Search Tool:
- To perform a comprehensive search across your computer and online, use the Search tool located on the Taskbar.
- Simply click the magnifier icon or press the Windows key + S on your keyboard.
- Enter your search query in the provided search box.
- You can apply filters like apps, documents, web, and more to refine your results.

- For specific searches within folders, such as locating a folder named Photos, you can use a syntax like folders: Photos in the search box.
- You can also customize Search settings and permissions to control the content included in your search results.

2. File Explorer:

- To search for files and folders within a specific location, utilize File Explorer.
- Open the folder where you want to conduct the search and click the search box in the top-right corner, or press Ctrl + F on your keyboard.
- Enter your search terms and press Enter.
- You can adjust the scope of your search using the Search options menu, allowing you to search only the current folder or its subfolders.

3. Advanced Criteria in File Explorer:

- For more precise searches with advanced criteria, access the Search tab within File Explorer.
- Open the folder where you wish to search and click the Search tab located on the ribbon.
- Here, you can employ various filters such as Date modified, Type, Size, Tags, and more to refine your search.
- Operators like AND, OR, NOT, and others can be used to combine multiple filters for specific search criteria.

4. Cortana Assistant:

- To search for files and folders using natural language, engage the Cortana assistant.
- Click the microphone icon on the Taskbar or activate Cortana by saying Hey Cortana if voice activation is enabled.

- Verbally ask Cortana in plain English for what you need, such as Show me my photos from last week or Find my resume document.
- Cortana will present the search results in a separate window, making it easy to access the information you're looking for.

How to Undo or Redo an Action

To perform undo or redo actions you have the option of using keyboard shortcuts or mouse functions. Below, you'll find some common methods for accomplishing these tasks:

Undoing an action can be achieved by pressing Ctrl+Z on your keyboard. Repeatedly pressing this combination allows you to undo multiple steps. Alternatively, you can click the Undo button located on the Quick Access Toolbar, which is represented by a curved arrow pointing to the left.

For redoing an action, press Ctrl+Y or F4 on your keyboard. If F4 doesn't trigger the redo function, you might need to press the F-Lock key or Fn key followed by F4. You can also use the Redo button on the Quick Access Toolbar, which is denoted by a hooked arrow pointing to the right. It's important to note that not all applications support the redo function.

To repeat an action, simply press Ctrl+Y or F4 on your keyboard. You can also access the Repeat button on the Quick Access Toolbar, which features a straight arrow pointing to the right. Keep in mind that certain actions, like using a function within an Excel cell, may not be eligible for repetition.

How to Recover a Deleted File folder

Recovering a deleted file folder on Windows 11 offers various methods, contingent on when and how the folder was deleted. Here are several potential approaches to consider:

1. Restore from Recycle Bin:

- The file folder was recently deleted and still resides in the Recycle Bin, simply open the Recycle Bin, right-click the folder, and select Restore. This action will return the folder to its original location.

2. Utilize File History for Permanent Deletions:

- In cases where you emptied the Recycle Bin or permanently deleted the folder using Shift+Delete, Windows 11 provides the option to recover files using the Restore Files feature.
- Access this feature by:
- Opening the Start menu and searching for Control Panel. Launch the Control Panel.
- Navigating to System and Security > File History.
- Click on Restore personal files from the left sidebar.
- Choose a backup copy from a point in time that contains the folder you wish to recover.
- Select the folder and click the green Restore button.

3. Recover from Previous Versions:

- If you lack a backup or haven't enabled File History, you can attempt recovery from a previous version. Windows automatically saves copies of files and folders as part of restore points.
- Follow these steps:

- Open File Explorer and go to the location where the folder resided before deletion.
- Right-click a space and select Properties.
- Click the Previous Versions tab.
- Choose a previous version that includes the folder you want to recover and click Restore.

4. Consider Third-Party Data Recovery Software:
- In instances where the above methods prove ineffective, resort to third-party data recovery software. Note that compatibility and reliability vary among such tools.
- One verified option for Windows 11 is Disk Drill. This software can scan your storage device and recover deleted files and folders of any format.
- Here's how to use Disk Drill:
- Download and install Disk Drill from its official website.
- Launch Disk Drill and select the drive where the folder was stored before deletion.
- Click the Search for lost data button and await completion of the scan.
- Preview the located files and folders, then select those you wish to recover.
- Click Recover and designate a secure location for saving the recovered files.

CONCLUSION

Windows File Explorer remains an indispensable tool in Windows 11, as it has been in previous versions of the operating system. File Explorer serves as the primary interface for managing files, folders, and storage devices, offering users a familiar and intuitive way to navigate their computer's file system.

Windows 11 has introduced several enhancements to File Explorer, including a refreshed and modernized user interface, streamlined navigation panes, and improved integration with cloud storage services like OneDrive. These updates make it easier for users to locate and organize their files, whether they are stored locally or in the cloud. File Explorer supports new productivity features such as Snap Layouts and Snap Groups, which allow for efficient multitasking and window management, enhancing the overall user experience.

Furthermore, it maintains backward compatibility, ensuring that users can access and manage legacy files and folders seamlessly while enjoying the benefits of the new features and design improvements.

As in previous versions, users can rely on File Explorer to perform essential file operations, including copying, moving, renaming, and deleting files and folders. Additionally, it offers advanced search capabilities and customization options, allowing users to put their file management experience to their specific needs.

CHAPTER SEVEN

HOW TO NAVIGATE ON THE WEB WITH WINDOWS 11

Introducing Microsoft Edge

Windows 11 comes equipped with Microsoft Edge as its default web browser, delivering a swift, secure, and browsing experience. Let's delve into the features and advantages of employing Microsoft Edge on this operating system:

1. **Chromium Engine Foundation**: Microsoft Edge is underpinned by the Chromium engine, ensuring extensive support for web standards and extensions. Additionally, you can seamlessly synchronize your settings, bookmarks, passwords, and browsing history across your various devices via your Microsoft account.

2. **Modern and Customizable Design**: The browser boasts a sleek and contemporary design that adapts to your preferences and requirements. You have the freedom to personalize your new tab page with diverse themes, layouts, and content. Also, you can efficiently manage your tabs using vertical tabs in a sidebar or group related tabs together for improved organization.

3. **Effortless Content Collection**: With the built-in Collections feature, collecting and organizing web content for later use is a breeze. You can create collections for a variety of topics such as travel plans, shopping lists, or research projects. Furthermore, you can export your collections to popular formats like Word, Excel, or PowerPoint with a single click.

4. **Intelligent Search Functionality**: Microsoft Edge offers a robust search function that expedites your quest for information. You can utilize the address bar to search the web, your browsing history, or even your device. Voice search is also at your disposal, allowing you to verbally articulate your queries. Additionally, the Bing sidebar provides immediate answers and information without navigating away from your current page.

5. **Comprehensive Security and Privacy**: Rest easy knowing that Microsoft Edge incorporates a wide array of security and privacy features to shield you from online threats and trackers. The InPrivate mode enables anonymous browsing with no traces left on your device. The Tracking Prevention feature empowers you to block unwanted trackers and ads. Furthermore, the Password Monitor feature ensures the safety of your credentials by checking for potential compromises and facilitating password changes.

6. **Productivity and Creativity Tools**: Enhance your productivity and creativity with an array of integrated tools and functionalities. The Web Capture tool simplifies screenshot-taking and web page annotations. The Immersive Reader tool provides a distraction-free reading mode with customizable text preferences and learning tools. Additionally, seamless integration with Microsoft 365 allows convenient access to your files and documents from OneDrive, Outlook, or Teams.

Using Multiple Tabs

Harnessing the power of multiple tabs in Windows 11 can transform your screen management and enhance your workspace efficiency. There are several methods to employ multiple tabs on Windows 11, catering to your specific preferences and requirements. Here's an overview of these techniques:

1. Snap Layouts for Window Organization:

- Utilize the Snap Layouts feature to partition your screen into two, three, or four distinct sections, facilitating seamless window organization. To activate Snap Layouts, simply hover your cursor over the maximize button of a window and select one of the available layout options. Additionally, you can adjust window sizes by dragging the dividing lines between them.

2. Snap Groups for Taskbar Convenience:

- Streamline your multitasking experience by creating Snap Groups, which allow you to group multiple windows for quick access via the taskbar. To establish a Snap Group, employ Snap Layouts to snap two or more windows, then hover over one of them in the taskbar to identify the group. You can also rename or close a Snap Group effortlessly by right-clicking on it within the taskbar.

3. Multiple Desktops for Task Segmentation:

- Enhance task and project management by making use of the Multiple Desktops feature. Generate separate desktop environments tailored to different tasks or projects. To initiate a new desktop, click the Task View icon in the taskbar and select New Desktop. Switching between desktops is effortless, either through Task View or via the keyboard shortcut Windows + Tab.

4. File Explorer Tabs for Streamlined Navigation:

- Elevate your file management experience with the Tabs feature in File Explorer. Activate Tabs by navigating to Settings > Windows Update and ensuring you have the latest updates installed. Once enabled, you can easily open multiple tabs in File

Explorer. Simply click the plus icon adjacent to the address bar or use the keyboard shortcut Ctrl + T to initiate a new tab.

Using Favorites

Introducing Favorites, a novel addition to Windows 11, offering the convenience of pinning your frequently used or essential files directly to the Home page of File Explorer. This feature streamlines access and management of your favorites, alongside an effortless search capability using the File Explorer search box. Here's a guide on how to make the most of favorites:

1. Adding Files to Favorites:

- To incorporate a file into your favorites, simply right-click on the desired file and choose Add to Favorites. Alternatively, you can employ the drag-and-drop method by moving the file to the Favorites section located on the Home page of File Explorer.

2. Removing Files from Favorites:

- When it's time to declutter your favorites, right-click on the file situated within the Favorites section and opt for Remove from Favorites. Alternatively, a quick drag-and-drop action outside the Favorites section accomplishes the same task.

3. Show or Hide the Favorites Section:

- Put your File Explorer interface by revealing or concealing the Favorites section. Click on the three-dot menu icon adjacent to Favorites and select either Hide or Show. Advanced users can also utilize a registry tweak to manipulate this setting for all users system-wide.

4. Clearing and Resetting Favorites:

- When the need arises to start anew with your favorites, you have a couple of options. You can use a command prompt or delete a specific registry key to clear and reset your favorites. This process effectively wipes all files from your favorites list and restores the default settings, offering a clean slate for organization.

Customizing Edge Settings

Customizing Microsoft Edge settings is a fantastic way to improve your web browsing experience for maximum personalization and convenience. You can effortlessly modify a variety of settings and preferences in Microsoft Edge, spanning from your homepage and search engine to appearance and privacy options. Here's a step-by-step guide to assist you in customizing Edge settings:

1. Accessing Edge Settings:
- Launch Microsoft Edge and locate the Settings and More button (depicted as three dots) situated in the upper-right corner of the browser window.

2. Opening Settings:
- Click on the Settings option from the dropdown menu that appears.

3. Exploring Categories:
- On the left-hand pane within the Settings window, you'll find an array of distinct categories encompassing various settings that can be adjusted to suit your preferences. These categories include Profiles, Privacy, Search and Services, Appearance, On Startup, and more.

4. Customizing Settings:
- Select the specific category you wish to customize, then explore the available options on the right-hand pane. For instance, if you desire to change your homepage, click on On Startup, and

opt for Open a specific page or pages. Subsequently, input the URL of the webpage you wish to set as your startup page.

5. Saving Changes:

- After making your desired modifications, you can simply close the Settings tab or click the Back button to return to the main Settings page. Rest assured that your changes will be saved automatically.

Additionally, you can further enhance your browsing experience by customizing the new tab page in Microsoft Edge, which is the page that greets you when opening a new tab or window. Here's how to do it:

1. Customizing the New Tab Page:

- Initiate Microsoft Edge and click the New Tab button (Ctrl + T keyboard shortcut).

2. Accessing Page Settings:

- Locate the Page settings menu, denoted by three dots, located in the top-right corner of the new tab page.

3. Selecting a Layout:

- Choose a page layout from the drop-down menu: Focused, Inspirational, or Informational. Each layout boasts a distinct design and content, including background images, quick links, and news headlines.

4. Custom Layout:

- Should none of the predefined layouts align with your preferences, you can opt for the Custom page layout. Within this option, you have the flexibility to enable or disable quick links, the image of the day, and manage your preferences for viewing Microsoft News content.

5. Language & Content Selection:

- Utilize the Language & Content drop-down menu to specify the language and region for the content you prefer to encounter when launching a new tab.

How to add a Bookmark

A bookmark is a convenient way to save a webpage for future reference, and you can easily add bookmarks using Microsoft Edge, the default web browser. Here's a straightforward guide to accomplish this task:

1. Accessing Microsoft Edge and the Desired Webpage:
- Begin by launching Microsoft Edge and navigating to the webpage you wish to bookmark.

2. Creating a Bookmark:
- In the address bar, locate and click on the star icon. This action will trigger a pop-up window where you can customize and organize your bookmark.

3. Customizing Bookmark Details:
- Within the pop-up window, you have the option to alter the name of the bookmark if desired, or you can retain the default title of the webpage.

4. Choosing a Bookmark Folder:
- You can also designate the folder in which you want to save your bookmark. If you prefer a new folder, you can create one by selecting New folder. The default folder for bookmarks is Favorites, which serves as the primary bookmark repository in Microsoft Edge.

5. Saving the Bookmark:
- Once you've determined the name and folder for your bookmark, simply click Done. Your bookmark will be securely

saved and readily accessible through the Favorites menu within Microsoft Edge.

How to show the Bookmarks Bar

The bookmarks bar in Microsoft Edge is a horizontal strip located just below the address bar, designed to showcase your saved bookmarks. To control its visibility on Windows 11, you can easily show or hide the bookmarks bar by following these straightforward steps:

1. Accessing Microsoft Edge Settings:

- Launch Microsoft Edge and locate the Settings and more button, represented by three dots, situated in the upper-right corner of the browser window.

2. Entering the Settings Menu:

- From the dropdown menu that appears, select Settings.

3. Navigating to Appearance Preferences:

- Within the left-hand pane of the Settings window, click on Appearance.

4. Customizing the Toolbar:

- In the right-hand pane, under the Customize toolbar section, locate the option labeled Show favorites bar. Here, you can toggle this option on or off to display or conceal the bookmarks bar based on your preference. Moreover, you have the option to exclusively display the favorites bar on new tabs.

How to set up a new Homepage

A homepage is a web page that you see when you open your web browser or a new tab, you can easily configure a new homepage using Microsoft Edge.

Here are the step-by-step instructions to achieve this:

1. Launch Microsoft Edge and Visit Your Desired Homepage:

- Begin by opening Microsoft Edge and navigating to the web page you wish to set as your homepage.

2. Access Microsoft Edge Settings:

- In the top-right corner of the browser window, locate and click on the Settings and more button, depicted as three dots.

3. Enter the Settings Menu:

- From the dropdown menu that appears, select Settings.

4. Navigating to Appearance Preferences:

- Within the left-hand pane of the Settings window, locate and click on Appearance.

5. Activate the Home Button:

- In the Appearance section, find the option labeled Show home button and toggle it on.

6. Specify Your Homepage:

- You now have two choices:
- Choose the New tab page if you prefer your browser to open with a blank new tab.
- Alternatively, select Enter URL to input the web address of the specific page you want to designate as your homepage.

View and Delete your browsing history.

Browsing history is a detailed log of the websites you've visited and the files you've downloaded while using your web browser. You can easily view and manage your browsing history using Microsoft Edge. Here are step-by-step instructions to help you with these tasks:

Viewing Your Browsing History:

1. Open Microsoft Edge and locate the Settings and more button (represented as three dots) in the upper-right corner of the browser window.
2. From the dropdown menu that appears, select History. Alternatively, you can use the keyboard shortcut Ctrl + H to open the History panel.
3. You'll be presented with a list of your browsing history entries, organized by date and time. You can scroll through this list or use the search box to find a specific entry. Additionally, you have the option to filter the list by type, such as websites, media, or downloads.

Deleting Your Browsing History:
1. To remove your browsing history, click on the Clear browsing data button located at the top of the History panel.
2. A pop-up window will appear, allowing you to select what you want to clear. You can also access this window directly using the keyboard shortcut Ctrl + Shift + Delete.
3. Under Time range, choose a time frame from the drop-down menu. Options include clearing data from All time, the Last hour, the Last 24 hours, the Last 7 days, or the Last 4 weeks.
4. Next, select the types of browsing data you wish to delete. You can customize this based on your preferences. For example, you might want to remove browsing history and cookies while retaining passwords and autofill form data.
5. Finally, click the Clear now button to confirm your selection. Your chosen browsing data will be promptly deleted from your device, or across all synced devices if you have synchronization enabled.

How to enable private browsing

Private browsing is a valuable feature that permits you to explore the web discreetly, leaving no traces of your online activity on your device or in your browsing history.

Microsoft Edge: Microsoft Edge refers to its private browsing mode as InPrivate. To activate InPrivate browsing in Microsoft Edge, you have several options:

1. Right-click on the Microsoft Edge logo in the taskbar and choose the New InPrivate window.
2. In Microsoft Edge, right-click on a link and select Open link in the InPrivate window.
3. Within Microsoft Edge, click on Settings and more (represented by three dots) in the top-right corner and opt for the New InPrivate window.
4. Alternatively, you can employ the keyboard shortcut Ctrl + Shift + N to open a new InPrivate window.

Activating private browsing mode in your web browser initiates a distinct window, typically marked with a unique icon or color, signifying that you are engaged in a private browsing session. You retain the flexibility to switch between standard and private browsing windows at your convenience. Nevertheless, it's vital to recognize that private browsing does not confer online anonymity nor safeguard you against potential threats like hackers or malware.

Private browsing primarily serves to inhibit your web browser from recording and storing data on your device, encompassing your browsing history, cookies, passwords, and related information. While it safeguards these aspects from local visibility, it's essential to understand that other entities, such as your internet service provider, educational institution, or workplace, and the websites you frequent, may still possess the capability to monitor and track your online activities.

In essence, private browsing offers a limited form of privacy, geared toward local data concealment, but it does not constitute a comprehensive shield against broader online surveillance or security threats.

How to Zoom in on a page

Zooming in on a page using Microsoft Edge offers various methods to cater to your preferences and requirements. Here are several approaches:

1. Keyboard Shortcuts for Precision:
- For precise control, employ keyboard shortcuts:
- To zoom in, press Ctrl + +, which increases the zoom level by 25% increments.
- To zoom out, use Ctrl + -, reducing the zoom level by 25%.
- To reset to the default 100% zoom level, press Ctrl + 0.

2. Mouse Wheel Convenience:
- Utilize the mouse wheel for a dynamic zooming experience:
- Hold down the Ctrl key while scrolling up to zoom in, incrementally increasing the zoom level by 5% with each scroll.
- Hold Ctrl and scroll down to zoom out, decreasing the zoom level similarly.

3. Menu Navigation for Quick Adjustments:
- Access the Settings and more button, denoted by three dots, situated in the upper-right corner of the browser window.

- From the menu that emerges, select either Zoom in or Zoom out. This method also adjusts the zoom level by 25% increments.

4. Default Zoom Level Setting:
- Put your browsing experience by setting a default zoom level for all websites in Microsoft Edge:
- Navigate to Settings and more > Settings.
- Click on Accessibility.
- Under Page zoom, select your preferred zoom level from the drop-down menu.

How to Block Ads

Blocking ads in Microsoft Edge on Windows 11 can be tailored to the type of ads you want to combat and your personal preferences. Here are various methods to achieve ad blocking:

Blocking Pop-up Ads:

1. To thwart pop-up ads that open new windows, tabs, or partial windows on top of your current web page, take advantage of the built-in pop-up blocker feature in Microsoft Edge. This feature is typically enabled by default, but you can verify or modify its settings by following these steps:
- Launch Microsoft Edge and locate the Settings and more button, represented as three dots, in the upper-right corner of the browser window.
- Select Settings from the ensuing menu.
- On the left-hand pane, click Cookies and site permissions.
- Under All permissions, locate and click on Pop-ups and redirects.
- Activate the Block (recommended) toggle.

Blocking In-Page Ads:

2. To combat ads that appear within web pages, including banners, videos, or sponsored links, you can employ browser extensions designed to block ads from various sources. One of the most renowned and effective extensions is AdBlock Plus, available for download and installation from the Microsoft Edge Add-ons store:

- Initiate Microsoft Edge and navigate to the AdBlock Plus page in the Microsoft Edge Add-ons store.
- Click on the Get button to incorporate the extension into your browser.
- Confirm your choice by clicking Add extension.

Once the extension is successfully installed, you'll spot a red ABP icon in your browser toolbar. This icon grants access to AdBlock Plus settings and options.

Whitelisting Trusted Websites:

3. If there are specific websites you wish to support or view ads from, you can add them to your whitelist in AdBlock Plus. Here's how:

- Open Microsoft Edge and access the AdBlock Plus extension page within the Microsoft Edge Add-ons store.
- Click on the Get button to add the extension to your browser.
- Confirm your selection by clicking Add extension.

Following the successful installation, the extension menu will allow you to whitelist chosen websites by selecting Don't run on this page.

How to Download a File

To download a file follow these steps:

1. Navigate to the Desired Web Page:

- Launch Microsoft Edge and visit the web page containing the file you wish to download.

2. Initiate the Download:

- Locate and click on either the file link or the download button associated with the desired file. This action will trigger a pop-up window, prompting you to specify how you want to handle the file.

3. Choose Your Download Option:

- In the pop-up window, you will be presented with the following download options:
- **Open**: This option immediately downloads the file to a temporary folder and opens it. The temporary folder typically clears itself upon starting a new browser session.
- **Save as**: Selecting this option opens the file explorer, enabling you to rename the file and choose the destination folder for saving.
- **Save**: By choosing this option, the file will be saved to your default download location, which is typically the Downloads folder on your PC. You can modify the default download location by navigating to Settings and More > Settings > Downloads and selecting Change next to Location.

4. Monitor Download Progress:

- Once you've made your selection, the file will commence downloading. You can track the progress and status of your downloads by clicking on the Downloads button in the toolbar. This button is recognizable as a downward arrow with a line beneath it. Alternatively, you can use the keyboard shortcut Ctrl + J to access the Downloads menu.

5. Access and Manage Downloads:

- When the download is completed, you have several options:
- Open the file.
- Open the folder where the file is saved.
- Delete the file from the Downloads menu.
- You can also perform more extensive management of your downloads by clicking on See more in the Downloads menu and selecting options such as Open folder, Clear all, or Manage.

Add-ons and Extension

Extensions and add-ons are convenient tools that enhance your browsing experience and provide you with greater control. Below, you'll find steps to assist you in adding, disabling, or uninstalling extensions in Microsoft Edge:

To Add an Extension from the Microsoft Store:
1. Launch Microsoft Edge and locate the Extensions icon, situated to the right of your browser's address bar.
2. Click on Extensions and then choose Open Microsoft Edge Add-ons.
3. Browse for the desired extension and click on Get.
4. Thoroughly review the permissions required by the extension, and if you're satisfied, click Add extension to proceed.

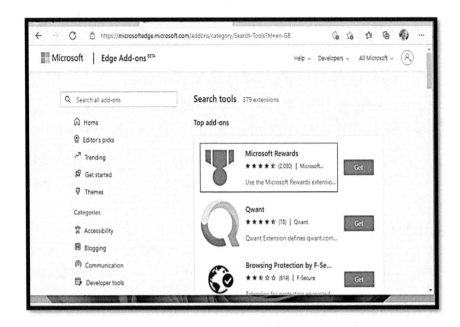

To Add an Extension from the Chrome Web Store:

1. Open Microsoft Edge and navigate to the Chrome Web Store.
2. In the banner at the top of the page, click Allow extensions from other stores and confirm by clicking Allow.
3. Find the extension you wish to add and click Add to Chrome.
4. Carefully review the permissions requested by the extension, and if you're comfortable, click Add extension to continue.

To Disable an Extension:

1. Launch Microsoft Edge and click on the Extensions icon beside your browser's address bar.
2. Select Manage extensions.
3. Locate the extension you want to disable and toggle the switch next to it.

To Remove an Extension:

1. Open Microsoft Edge and click on the Extensions icon next to your browser's address bar.
2. Select More actions next to the extension you wish to remove.

3. Then, choose Remove from Microsoft Edge and confirm the removal.

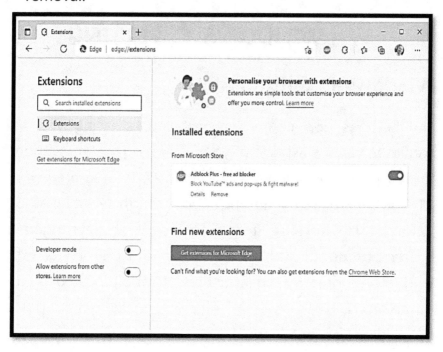

CONCLUSION

Microsoft Edge represents a powerful, secure, and feature-rich web browsing solution. Its integration with the Windows ecosystem, emphasis on performance and security, and ongoing development efforts make it a compelling choice for users seeking a reliable and efficient web browser on their Windows 11 devices. Whether for work, research, or leisure, Microsoft Edge continues to provide a versatile and enjoyable web browsing experience. Web browser that continues to evolve and improve, offering users a compelling browsing experience.

CHAPTER EIGHT

WINDOWS 11 SETTINGS

Windows 11 Setting App

The Settings app comes pre-installed, allowing you to use and configure various aspects of your operating system without the need for a separate download, as it's seamlessly integrated with Windows 11. You can access the Settings app through several methods:

1. Keyboard Shortcut: Press the Windows + I keys together.

2. Start Menu: Click the Start button and then choose the Settings icon (represented by a gear-shaped symbol) located on the left side of the menu.

3. Taskbar Context Menu:

- Right-click the Taskbar.
- Select Taskbar settings from the context menu.

4. Quick Settings on Taskbar:

- Click the Quick Settings button on the right side of the Taskbar (featuring battery, network, and volume icons).
- Choose Settings from the flyout menu.

5. Search:

- Utilize the Start menu or the search box on the Taskbar.
- Search for Settings and click on the top result.

The Settings app boasts a refreshed design and layout, categorizing options into various sections and subcategories. It empowers you to modify settings related to personalization, system preferences, Bluetooth, network configurations, app management, account settings, privacy controls, gaming preferences, accessibility features, and more. Furthermore, you can efficiently oversee and manage the permissions granted to each installed app directly from within the Settings app.

System Settings

System Settings offer the flexibility to adjust various settings such as Display, Sound, Notifications, Power, Storage, Multitasking, Activation, Troubleshooting, Recovery, and more.

Bluetooth and Devices

The Bluetooth and device functionality are at your disposal, providing you with the means to establish connections and oversee wireless peripherals for your PC. Within the Bluetooth and devices settings, you can effortlessly perform tasks like pairing, unpairing, enabling, disabling, or addressing issues with your Bluetooth devices. This includes a wide range of devices such as keyboards, mice, speakers, headphones, printers, scanners, and more.

Additionally, the Bluetooth and device settings offer the flexibility to incorporate or detach other hardware peripherals like USB drives, monitors, cameras, microphones, and similar devices, enhancing the versatility and convenience of your experience. Launch the Settings app, and navigate to Bluetooth & devices in the left sidebar to access a comprehensive array of options and features. Here, you'll find the following capabilities:

1. **Bluetooth Toggle**: Adjacent to the Bluetooth option, there's a convenient toggle switch that allows you to swiftly enable or disable Bluetooth connectivity.

2. **Adding New Devices**: By selecting Add device, you can initiate the pairing process for either a fresh Bluetooth device or another type of peripheral to connect with your PC.

3. **Managing Paired Devices**: Under various categories such as Audio, Mouse, Keyboard & Pen, and more, you'll discover a list of all your paired devices. Clicking on any of these devices grants you access to additional details and the option to remove them from your setup.

4. **Efficient Search**: At the top of the page, a search box is available, enabling you to quickly locate specific devices or settings within the Bluetooth & devices section.

Enabling Bluetooth connectivity in your Windows 11 Computer

To activate Bluetooth connectivity, adhere to these steps:

1. Enable Bluetooth:

- Toggle Bluetooth On via Settings: Click on the Bluetooth toggle switch to enable it. Alternatively, you can access the Quick Settings menu on the right side of the taskbar and click on the Bluetooth icon to turn it on.

2. Pair Your Device:

- In the Bluetooth & devices settings, click on the Add device button. This action will display a list of available devices currently in pairing mode.
- Select the desired device you wish to connect and follow the on-screen instructions to complete the pairing process.

3. Swift Pair (if supported):

- If your device supports Swift Pair, you will receive a notification when it's within proximity and set to pairing mode.
- Simply click on the notification to swiftly pair the device without further configuration.

Turning the Bluetooth on via Settings Menu

To activate Bluetooth, follow these simple steps:

1. Open the Settings app.
2. Select Bluetooth & devices from the options on the left side of the screen to access your computer's Bluetooth and device settings.
3. Toggle the Bluetooth switch to the On position. You'll know it's active when a blue checkmark appears.

Turning the Bluetooth on via Action Center

To ensure that the Bluetooth icon appears in the Action Center, follow these steps:

1. Access Settings: Click the Start button in the lower-left corner of your screen, represented by the Windows logo. Then, select Settings.

2. Navigate to Devices: Inside the Settings menu, click on Devices. This option controls various hardware-related settings on your computer.

3. Bluetooth & Other Devices: In the Devices section, you will find Bluetooth & other devices on the left sidebar. Click on it.

4. More Bluetooth Options: Under the Related settings section on the right-hand side, you'll see an option labeled More Bluetooth Options. Click on this option to access additional Bluetooth settings.

5. Options Tab: Within the Bluetooth settings window, select the Options tab. This tab provides various Bluetooth configuration options.

6. Enable Bluetooth Icon: To enable the Bluetooth icon in the notification area (Action Center), check the box that says Show the Bluetooth icon in the notification area.

How to Pair Bluetooth Devices to your Windows 11 computer

Certainly! Here's a step-by-step guide on how to add a Bluetooth device to your PC running Windows 11:

1. Open Settings: Click the Start button (the Windows logo in the lower-left corner of your screen) to access the Start menu. Then, select Settings to open the Settings app.

2. Devices: Inside the Settings app, you'll find various options. Look for and click on Devices. This section is where you manage your PC's hardware and peripherals.

3. Access Bluetooth & Other Devices: In the Devices menu on the left-hand side, click on Bluetooth & other devices. This is where you manage your Bluetooth connections and other device-related settings.

4. Add a Bluetooth Device: Under the Bluetooth & other devices section, locate and click on the Add Bluetooth or other device option. This initiates the process of adding a new Bluetooth device.

5. Choose Bluetooth: A new window will appear with a list of device types you can add. Select Bluetooth from this list. Your PC will now start searching for nearby Bluetooth devices that are in pairing mode.

6. Select the Device: After a moment, your PC will display a list of available Bluetooth devices. Choose the device you want to connect to from the list. If the device is not on the list, make sure it's in pairing mode, and your PC will detect it.

7. Follow Additional Instructions (if needed): Depending on the type of device you're connecting, you may need to follow additional instructions. These instructions can include entering a PIN or confirming a pairing code on the device itself.

8. Select Done: Once your PC successfully pairs with the Bluetooth device, you'll receive a confirmation message. Click Done to complete the process.

Disconnecting or Removing a Bluetooth Devices from your Windows 11 Pc

To disconnect or remove a Bluetooth device, follow these straightforward steps:

Disconnecting a Bluetooth Device:

1. Utilize the Quick Settings Menu: On the right side of the taskbar, you'll find the Quick Settings menu. Click on the Bluetooth icon to access a list of your paired devices. Simply select the device you wish to disconnect. Alternatively, you can turn off the Bluetooth toggle switch to disconnect all connected devices at once.

Removing a Bluetooth Device:

1. Navigate to Settings: Open the Settings app.
2. Access Bluetooth & Devices: Click on Bluetooth & devices.
3. Select the Device: Identify the Bluetooth device you want to remove and click on it.
4. Remove Device: Choose the Remove device option, and confirm your decision. Alternatively, you can also employ the Device Manager to uninstall the device from your PC.

How to use the Bluetooth Device Wizard

The Bluetooth Device Wizard is a valuable tool that facilitates the connection and management of your Bluetooth devices. Whether you need to pair, unpair, or troubleshoot devices like keyboards, mice, speakers, headphones, printers, or scanners, the Bluetooth Device Wizard simplifies the process. Here are detailed steps to assist you in utilizing the Bluetooth Device Wizard effectively:

Opening the Bluetooth Device Wizard:

- To access the Bluetooth Device Wizard, initiate a search by typing devicepairingwizard in the taskbar's search box. Select the wizard from the top search result. This opens the classic pairing wizard, which automatically searches for available Bluetooth devices.

Pairing a Bluetooth Device:

- To pair a Bluetooth device, ensure that the device is in pairing mode, powered on, and set to discoverable. The specific method for making a device discoverable varies by device type; consult the device's documentation or the manufacturer's website for guidance.

- From the list of available devices displayed, select the device you wish to connect. Follow the on-screen instructions to complete the pairing process.

- If your device supports Swift Pair, you'll receive a notification when it's nearby and in pairing mode. Click on the notification to expedite the pairing process.

Unpairing a Bluetooth Device:

- Navigate to Settings and then Bluetooth & devices.
- Click on the device you want to remove, and then select Remove device. Confirm your choice.

- Alternatively, you can use the Device Manager to uninstall the device from your PC.

Troubleshooting a Bluetooth Device:

- In Settings, go to Bluetooth & devices and select Troubleshoot under Related settings.
- Choose your device from the list and follow the provided steps to address and resolve any issues.
- You can also employ the Bluetooth troubleshooter by typing msdt.exe -id DeviceDiagnostic in the Run dialog (accessible by pressing Windows + R) and then hitting Enter.

Network and Internet

Network and Internet functionalities are essential features that empower you to establish and manage your online connectivity and settings. Within the Network and Internet settings, you can put a wide range of network-related options to suit your needs. These settings encompass:

- **Wi-Fi Configuration**: You can set up and customize your Wi-Fi connections, including connecting to networks, managing saved networks, and adjusting Wi-Fi preferences.
- **Ethernet Settings**: Configure Ethernet connections and manage Ethernet-related parameters.
- **VPN Configuration**: Easily set up and customize Virtual Private Network (VPN) connections to enhance your online security and privacy.
- **Mobile Hotspot**: Create and manage mobile hotspot connections, allowing you to share your device's internet connection with other devices.

- **Airplane Mode**: Enable or disable Airplane mode for convenient control over wireless communications.
- **Proxy Settings**: Configure proxy server settings to customize your internet access and enhance privacy.

These Network and Internet settings also provide the tools necessary for network management and troubleshooting:

- **Network Status Check**: Monitor and assess your network status to ensure a stable and reliable internet connection.
- **Troubleshooting**: Access troubleshooting tools and guides to diagnose and resolve connectivity issues.
- **Network Setup**: Set up new networks or establish connections as needed, ensuring seamless online access.

Opening Network and Internet Settings

- Access the Start Menu: Click on the Start button in the lower-left corner of your screen.
- Select Settings: locate Settings and select it. This action will open the Settings app.

Navigate to Network & Internet:

- Inside the Settings app, you'll see various categories on the left-hand side. Look for and click on Network & internet. This category deals with all your network and internet-related settings.
- Access Network and Internet Settings: Once you've selected Network & internet, you'll be directed to a screen displaying various network-related options. Here, you can configure and manage settings like Wi-Fi, Ethernet, VPN, proxy, and more.

Personalization

Accessing Personalization

1. Desktop Right-Click (or Select and Hold):

- Begin by going to your desktop, which is the main screen you see after logging in.
- To access Personalization options, right-click anywhere on the desktop. Alternatively, if you are using a touchscreen device, you can select and hold your finger on an empty area of the desktop.

2. Choose Personalize:

- After right-clicking or selecting and holding, a context menu will appear. Among the options presented, you will find Personalize. Click on Personalize to proceed.

3. Explore Personalization Options:

- Clicking Personalize will open the Personalization settings in Windows 11. Here, you can customize various aspects of your desktop and user interface, including:
- **Themes**: Change your system's theme to alter the overall look and feel of your desktop.
- **Backgrounds**: Set your desktop background or wallpaper with your choice of images or slideshows.
- **Colors**: Customize the accent color and appearance of various UI elements.
- **Lock Screen**: Adjust your lock screen background and settings.
- **Start Menu**: Tailor the appearance of the Start menu, including its layout and design.
- **Taskbar**: Modify the look and behavior of the taskbar.
- **Sound**: Adjust sound settings and choose your system's audio scheme.
- **Accessibility**: Configure accessibility settings to suit your needs.

- **Other options**: Depending on the Windows 11 version and updates, you may have additional personalization options available.

Apps

Applications, or apps, are versatile software tools that enable you to perform a wide array of tasks, encompassing activities like web browsing, gaming, photo editing, music playback, and beyond. Windows 11 accommodates various types of apps, each serving a distinct purpose:

1. Windows Apps: These applications are meticulously crafted for Windows 11, harnessing the latest OS features and technologies. To acquire Windows apps, you can conveniently browse and download them from the revamped Microsoft Store, which offers an enhanced interface and a curated selection of top-quality apps. Notable examples of Windows apps include Microsoft Edge, Microsoft Office, Microsoft Teams, Paint 3D, and Your Phone.

2. Android Apps: introduces the capability to run Android apps on your PC, extending compatibility beyond smartphones and tablets. This feature is made possible through the Amazon App Store and Intel Bridge technology. You can access a curated collection of Android apps directly from the Microsoft Store and effortlessly install them on your computer. Prominent Android apps available on Windows 11 include TikTok, Disney+, Adobe Photoshop Elements, and more.

3. Web Apps: Web apps operate within your web browser, eliminating the need for installation or local storage on your PC. Despite their browser-based nature, web apps can deliver comparable functionality and performance to native apps while offering enhanced accessibility and cross-platform compatibility. You can use web apps by simply visiting their respective websites or pinning them to your taskbar or start menu. Examples of web apps encompass Gmail, Spotify, Netflix, and numerous others.

Accounts

User accounts represent distinct user profiles that you can create and oversee on your computer. These accounts grant individuals their personalized sign-in credentials, files, preferences, and settings. Additionally, they allow you to share your computer with others by creating dedicated accounts. Windows 11 accommodates various types of user accounts, each put for specific needs:

1. Microsoft Accounts: These accounts are associated with a Microsoft email address and password, such as Outlook.com, Hotmail.com, or Live.com. Alternatively, you can use an email address from another provider like Gmail or Yahoo to create a Microsoft account. Microsoft accounts provide access to a wide array of Microsoft online services, including OneDrive, Office, Skype, Xbox, and more. They also enable features such as sync settings, Windows Hello, and device backup.

2. Local Accounts: Local accounts are not linked to any online service. They necessitate only a username and password for sign-in. These accounts offer enhanced privacy and security, but they may not provide the same integrated benefits as Microsoft accounts.

3. Work or School Accounts: These accounts are furnished by your organization or educational institution. They facilitate access to domain-specific resources and services, such as email, network drives, SharePoint sites, and others. Additionally, they enforce policies and configurations set by your administrator.

4. Child Accounts: Child accounts are designed for users under the age of 13 and require parental or guardian management through the Microsoft Family Safety app. These accounts include parental control features such as screen time restrictions, content filtering, location tracking, and more.

To manage and oversee user accounts on your PC, you can utilize the Settings app:

- Click the Start button and select the gear icon on the left side of the menu to access the Settings app.
- Alternatively, you can press the Windows + I keys on your keyboard to swiftly open the Settings app.
- Within the Settings app, navigate to the Accounts section, where you'll find a range of options and features for your user account and other users.
- Utilize the search box at the top to quickly locate specific account-related settings or features.

Time and Language

Time and Language settings encompass a suite of options and features that empower users to fine-tune and personalize their computer's date, time, language, and regional configurations. These settings facilitate precise adjustments and customization, offering control over several key aspects of your PC's environment. With the Time and Language settings, you can effortlessly:

- **Change Display Language**: Modify the language in which your Windows interface is presented, enabling you to work comfortably in your preferred language.
- **Adjust Keyboard Layout**: Put your keyboard layout to match your input preferences, ensuring a seamless typing experience.

- **Set Time Zone**: Specify your geographical time zone or enable automatic time zone detection to maintain accurate local time.
- **Customize Date and Time Format**: Personalize the way dates and times are displayed on your system, conforming to your regional or stylistic preferences.
- **Configure Regional Format**: Define how numbers, currency, dates, and times are formatted on your PC to align with your regional standards and conventions.

To modify the default language follow these steps:

- Access Settings: Open the Settings app.
- Navigate to Time & Language: In the Settings app, locate and click on the Time & language option.
- Select Language & Region: Within the Time & language section, click on Language & region.
- Add a New Language: In the Language section, locate and click the Add a language button situated under the Preferred languages setting.
- Search for the Desired Language: In the search field, enter the name of the new language you want to add and select it from the search results.

Proceed with Language Setup: After selecting your desired language, click the Next button to initiate the language setup process.

Gaming

Gaming delivers an exhilarating and immersive experience, harnessing the latest advancements in operating system technology. Windows 11 caters to a diverse array of gaming genres, including Windows-native games, Android games, and web-based games, offering elevated graphics quality, enhanced performance, and superior compatibility. The Windows 11 gaming ecosystem is complemented by a thriving community and convenient quick settings to keep you fully immersed in your gaming adventures. Here are some key highlights of gaming:

1. Game Mode: This feature optimizes your PC's performance for gaming by prioritizing your game's resources while reducing background activities. You can activate Game Mode by navigating to Settings > Gaming > Game Mode and toggle it on.

2. DirectX 12 Ultimate: Utilizing cutting-edge technology, DirectX 12 Ultimate replicates real-world lighting behaviors, resulting in lifelike game environments with realistic reflections, shadows, and refractions. It also supports advanced gaming features such as ray tracing, variable rate shading, mesh shaders, and sampler feedback.

3. Auto HDR: Automatically enhancing game visuals, Auto HDR enriches colors and contrast, delivering vibrant and realistic graphics. This feature is compatible with titles that utilize the DirectX 11 or later API and require an HDR-capable monitor.

4. DirectStorage: With DirectStorage, games load faster, and expansive virtual worlds become more accessible. To leverage this technology, you'll need an NVMe SSD for storing and running games using the Standard NVM Express Controller driver, in addition to a DirectX 12 GPU with Shader Model 6.0 support.

5. Xbox Game Pass: Xbox Game Pass is a subscription service granting you access to a vast library of over 100 PC games, including day-one releases, for a nominal monthly fee. It also enables online multiplayer gaming with friends and provides exclusive member discounts and deals.

6. Android Apps: A groundbreaking feature that enables the execution of Android apps on your PC using Amazon Appstore and

Intel Bridge technology. You can explore and install a selection of Android games directly from the Microsoft Store to enhance your gaming repertoire.

7. Game Bar: Game Bar is a versatile tool that grants you seamless access to various gaming features and settings without interrupting your gameplay. You can invoke Game Bar by pressing the Windows logo key + G on your keyboard. Game Bar facilitates tasks such as chatting with friends, recording clips, streaming gameplay, monitoring performance, controlling music playback, and more.

Accessibility

Accessibility is a topic that covers the various features and settings that are designed to make the operating system more inclusive and user-friendly for people with different needs and preferences.

Some of the accessibility features are:

1. **Narrator**: This built-in screen reader audibly conveys on-screen text and elements, extending support for braille devices.
2. **Color Filters**: It offers the flexibility to apply different color schemes like grayscale, inverted, or red-green, assisting those with color vision deficiencies.
3. **Contrast Themes**: Users can choose from a selection of high-contrast themes, enhancing the visibility of text and applications.
4. **Magnifie**r: This tool zooms in on-screen content while offering additional options such as color inversion, edge smoothing, and a reading mode.
5. **Live Captions**: Automatically transcribing spoken content from various sources like videos, apps, or microphones into text captions.

6. **Customizable Captions**: Users can customize and adjust caption styles for media content, including videos, TV shows, and movies.

7. **Single-Channel Audio**: Combines audio from both left and right channels into a single channel for an improved listening experience through speakers or headphones.

8. **Voice Access**: Empowers users to control their PC through voice commands, enabling tasks like app navigation, web browsing, email management, and more.

9. **Eye Control:** This feature facilitates PC and app navigation using eye-tracking technology, employing a straightforward launch pad interface.

10. **Voice Typing**: Users can compose documents or emails using their voice, leveraging AI to convert spoken words into text and punctuate as needed.

11. **Immersive Reader**: Enhances online reading fluency, comprehension, and focus with options such as read-aloud, text spacing, line focus, picture dictionaries, and translation support.
    Utilizing the Start menu and keyboard shortcuts provides users with convenient ways to access and customize accessibility features. Here's a detailed explanation of how to access these settings:

Using the Start Menu:

1. **Accessing the Start Menu**: To initiate this method, begin by selecting the Start button, which is represented by a four-square icon, typically located on your taskbar. It's a familiar starting point for many users.

2. **Navigating to Settings**: Once you click on the Start button, you'll see a menu pop up. From here, locate and select the Settings

option. The Settings menu is represented by a gear-shaped icon and is where you can customize various aspects of your experience.

3. **Accessing Accessibility Settings**: Within the Settings menu, you'll find an array of options for configuring your system. To access the accessibility features, look for and select Accessibility. It's usually categorized under sections like System or Accessibility & ease of use. By clicking on this option, you gain access to a comprehensive set of features that cater to vision, hearing, and interaction preferences.

4. **Making Customizations**: Within the Accessibility settings, you'll discover a wealth of options designed to meet your specific accessibility needs. You can adjust settings related to vision, hearing, and interaction preferences based on your requirements. This interface provides an organized and user-friendly way to fine-tune your experience.

Using the Keyboard Shortcut:

1. **Pressing the Windows Logo Key + U**: This method is perfect for users who prefer keyboard shortcuts. To open the Ease of Access settings window swiftly, press the Windows logo key (typically located next to the Ctrl key on your keyboard) and the letter U simultaneously.

2. **Navigating with Keyboard Commands**: Once the Ease of Access settings window appears, you can further navigate through the options using keyboard commands. The Tab key is used to move between different settings and controls, while the arrow keys (up, down, left, and right) allow you to select and adjust specific accessibility features. This keyboard-centric approach streamlines the process for users who are more comfortable with keyboard interactions.

Alternate input Devices

Alternative input devices encompass both hardware and software solutions designed to enable users with diverse impairments to interact with a computer using unconventional methods. These alternative input devices empower individuals to access a computer in a manner that suits their unique needs, including the use of their feet, head, eyes, mouth, breath, thumb, or a single finger. These devices exhibit a wide range of activation mechanisms, some responsive to physical motion, while others can be manipulated using nerve or muscle signals, optical tracking, and even brain activity and cognitive energy.

Alternate input methods offer users diverse ways to interact with their PCs, including voice, eye gaze, touch, or gestures. Windows 11 is equipped to support a wide array of alternate input devices, such as:

Microphones: Users can employ microphones for various functions, such as issuing voice commands, utilizing voice typing, or enabling live captions. Windows 11 features a built-in voice access capability, facilitating control of the PC via voice commands for tasks like app management, web browsing, email correspondence, and more. Voice typing allows users to compose documents or emails using their voice, harnessing AI to convert speech into text and punctuate accordingly. Additionally, live captions automatically transcribe spoken content from any audio source, including videos, apps, or microphones, rendering it as text captions.

Cameras: Cameras can be utilized to facilitate eye gaze and gestures. Windows 11 incorporates an integrated eye control feature, permitting users to navigate their PC and applications using eye-tracking-enabled cameras along with an intuitive launch pad. Gesture-based control enables users to manipulate their PC via hand movements, encompassing actions such as swiping, pinching, or tapping. Windows 11 supports a variety of gesture-enabled devices, including touchscreens, touchpads, and styluses.

Numeric Keypads: Numeric keypads serve as input mechanisms for mouse movements and clicks. Windows 11 includes a built-in mouse keys feature, enabling users to manage their mouse using a numeric keypad. Furthermore, the on-screen keyboard is available for users to select keys through mouse input or another pointing device like a joystick. It also offers a single switch mode for cycling through on-screen keys.

Other Devices: Users have the flexibility to employ a range of compatible devices for data input or command execution. For instance, steering wheels, VR headsets, game controllers, and braille devices can be utilized to enhance the gaming experience or facilitate accessibility features to individual needs.

Privacy and Security

Privacy and security are important aspects of the operating system that help users protect their personal data, devices, and online activities. Features and settings that can enhance the privacy and security of users, such as:

1. **Windows Security:** This integral application furnishes comprehensive protection against a spectrum of threats, including malware, ransomware, phishing attempts, and more. Windows Security encompasses additional functionalities such as Firewall management, device performance and health monitoring, family-oriented options, and additional security features.

2. **Privacy Settings:** Within the Settings app, users can access a dedicated section that affords them control over the extent of information they wish to share with Microsoft and other applications. Users can manage permissions for various data types, including those related to the camera, microphone, location, contacts, and more.

3. **Windows Hello:** This feature empowers users to access their devices securely through biometric authentication methods, including facial recognition, fingerprint scanning, and iris authentication. Additionally, Windows Hello provides alternative sign-in options, such as PINs and security keys, ensuring versatile yet robust device access.

4. **BitLocker:** BitLocker offers a formidable layer of protection by encrypting data on the device's hard drive, rendering it inaccessible to unauthorized individuals and potential hackers. Beyond

safeguarding the main hard drive, BitLocker extends its encryption capabilities to include removable drives like USB flash drives and external hard disks, bolstering data security across various storage mediums.

5. **Windows Update:** Windows Update operates as a vital mechanism that automates the download and installation of the latest security patches and feature updates for Windows 11, as well as other Microsoft products. Users possess the flexibility to pause updates or schedule their installation, ensuring that the operating system remains up-to-date and secure while accommodating individual preferences.

Windows Update

Windows Update is a feature that automatically downloads and installs the latest security patches and feature updates for Windows 11 and other Microsoft products. Windows Update also allows users to pause updates or choose when to install them.

To update Windows 11, you can follow these steps:

1. **Accessing Settings**: Open the Settings menu by pressing the Windows logo key and I on your keyboard or right-clicking the Start button and selecting Settings from the displayed list.

2. **Navigating to Windows Update**: Within the Settings menu, navigate to the Windows Update option located in the sidebar.

3. **Checking for Updates**: Once in the Windows Update settings, initiate the update process by clicking the Check for Updates button. This action prompts the system to search for available updates.

4. **Automatic Installation**: Should any updates be available, Windows 11 will automatically download and install them. In certain cases, a system restart may be required to finalize the installation.

5. **Preview Updates (Optional)**: If you encounter a Download and install option, it provides the opportunity to apply a preview of an upcoming Windows 11 update.

Additionally, you possess the ability to manage your update preferences and options within the Windows Update settings, including:

- **Viewing Update History**: Gain insights into the specifics of updates that have been installed on your PC.

- **Pause Updates**: Temporarily suspend the reception of updates for a period of up to 35 days, allowing you to maintain control over your update schedule.

- **Advanced Options**: Customize how updates are delivered, select the timing for update installations, and enable or disable optional updates, providing you with comprehensive control over your update experience.

CONCLUSION

The Settings app's Bluetooth and Devices, as well as Network and Internet sections, are essential components for managing hardware connections and network settings. They empower users to customize their computing experience, troubleshoot problems efficiently, and ensure their devices and network connections are secure and efficient. These settings are integral to creating a personalized and reliable computing environment in Windows 11.

CHAPTER NINE

EMAILING WITH FAMILY AND FRIENDS

The Windows Mail App

The Windows Mail app serves as an integrated email management tool, allowing users to effectively handle their emails from various accounts and services. With the Windows Mail app, you can seamlessly send, receive, and organize your emails while also gaining access to your calendar and contacts. Although it shares similarities with its Windows 10 counterpart, the Windows Mail app in Windows 11 introduces several new features and enhancements, including:

1. New Design: The Windows Mail app boasts a contemporary and streamlined design that aligns with the aesthetics of Windows 11. Users can further personalize the app with themes, colors, and fonts to match their individual style preferences.

2. Focused Inbox: This feature aids in email prioritization by categorizing messages into two tabs: Focused and Other. The Focused tab presents the most crucial emails, while the Other tab houses the rest. Users have the flexibility to switch between tabs or deactivate the feature through settings.

3. Swipe Actions: The Windows Mail app simplifies email management by enabling users to perform quick actions through left or right swipes. Action options include delete, archive, flag, mark as read or unread, move, or snooze, with customization available in the settings.

4. Multiple Accounts: Supporting a multitude of email accounts across various webmail services such as Gmail, Outlook.com, Yahoo!,

Office 365, and Exchange, the Windows Mail app facilitates easy addition or removal of accounts in the settings. Users can effortlessly switch between these accounts via the sidebar.

5. Linked Inboxes: This functionality permits the amalgamation of multiple inboxes into one, providing a unified view of emails from diverse accounts in a single location. Linked inboxes can be created or removed through the settings.

6. Calendar and Contacts Integration: The Windows Mail app seamlessly integrates with the Calendar and People apps on Windows 11, streamlining event and contact management within the app. Additionally, users can sync their calendars and contacts with external services like Google or iCloud.

To utilize the Windows Mail app ensure that your PC meets the minimum device specifications. You can verify your PC's compatibility by utilizing the PC Health Check app. Furthermore, you have the flexibility to explore a diverse range of PC and laptop options to your needs.

To begin using the Windows Mail app follow these steps:

1. Open the Windows Mail app by clicking the envelope icon on your taskbar or searching for it in the Start menu.
2. If you're using the app for the first time, a welcome screen will appear. Click Get started to proceed.
3. Select the email account you wish to add to the app. If your account isn't listed, click Add account.
4. Enter your email address and password, and follow the on-screen instructions to complete the setup.
5. Repeat steps 3 and 4 for any additional email accounts you want to add to the app.

Setting Up a New Email Account

To add a new email account, follow these steps:

1. Click on the Start button, type Mail into the search bar, and select the Mail app from the search results.
2. If this is your first time using the Mail app, a Welcome page will appear.
3. Click on Add account.
4. Choose the type of account you wish to add (e.g., Outlook, Gmail, Yahoo, etc.).
5. Enter the necessary account information and select Sign in.
6. Once the setup is complete, click Done.

Advanced Setup

Advanced setup in the Mail app offers users the flexibility to add an email account using customized configurations, including server addresses, port numbers, encryption preferences, and authentication methods. This option becomes particularly useful when your email account isn't supported by the standard automatic setup or when you wish to modify default settings.

To access the advanced setup feature within the Mail app, you can follow these steps:

1. Open the Mail app by either clicking on the envelope icon located on your taskbar or by searching for it in the Start menu.
2. If this marks your initial usage of the app, you'll encounter a welcome screen. Simply click Get started to proceed.
3. Select Advanced setup from the list of available options. You might need to scroll down to locate it.

4. Opt for the type of account you intend to add. You can choose between Exchange ActiveSync or Internet email. Unless your administrator specifically instructs you to use Exchange ActiveSync, it's recommended to select Internet email.

5. Proceed by entering the essential account information, which includes your email address, password, account name, and settings related to sending and receiving messages. You'll also be required to input details such as incoming and outgoing email server addresses, port configurations, as well as encryption and authentication preferences. This specific information can typically be obtained from your email provider or administrator.

6. To conclude the setup process, click Sign in.

Adding Multiple Email Account

If you wish to incorporate multiple email accounts into your PC, you have the option of utilizing either the built-in Mail app or the new Outlook app. Both applications offer the convenience of managing emails from diverse accounts and services within a single interface. Below are the steps to add multiple email accounts to each of these apps:

Adding Multiple Email Accounts to the Mail App:

1. Open the Mail app by clicking the envelope icon on your taskbar or by searching for it in the Start menu.

2. Click Get started to proceed.

3. Choose an email account that you intend to add to the app. If your account isn't listed, click Add account.

4. Enter your email address and password, then follow the on-screen instructions to complete the setup.

5. Repeat steps 3 and 4 for any additional email accounts you wish to integrate into the app.

Adding Multiple Email Accounts to the New Outlook App:

1. Launch the new Outlook app by clicking the calendar icon on your taskbar or searching for it in the Start menu.
2. Click on the Settings (gear) button located in the top-right corner.
3. Select Accounts.
4. Click on Email accounts.
5. Choose the Add account option.
6. Confirm your additional email account from providers such as Outlook.com, Gmail, Yahoo, or iCloud. You may be required to sign in using your credentials.
7. Click the Continue button.
8. Repeat steps 5 to 7 for any other email accounts you wish to include in the app.

Using the Mail App

To launch the Mail app, you have a couple of options. Simply click on the envelope icon conveniently located on your taskbar, or if you prefer, search for it in the Start menu.

When it comes to adding an email account to the Mail app, follow these steps:

- If you're using the Mail app for the first time, click Get started to initiate the setup. Alternatively, for those who are already acquainted with the app, click on the gear icon situated at the bottom-left corner and select Manage accounts.
- Now, pick the email account you wish to integrate into the app. You have the flexibility to choose from popular email services like Outlook.com, Gmail, Yahoo!, or iCloud. In case your specific

account isn't listed, don't fret; simply click Add account and opt for the Advanced setup option.

- Next, you'll be prompted to enter your email address and password. Follow the on-screen instructions meticulously to finalize the setup. This procedure can be repeated to add multiple email accounts to the Mail app, providing you with consolidated access.

To switch between your email accounts within the Mail app, just click on the account name conveniently displayed in the left sidebar. If you prefer a unified view, you can also create or remove linked inboxes, allowing you to access emails from different accounts all in one place. For reading or responding to emails, you can accomplish it by clicking on the respective email in the list of messages. Moreover, you can expedite actions on your emails with swift swipe actions—simply swipe left or right to choose from actions like delete, archive, flag, mark as read or unread, move, or snooze. These swipe actions can also be personalized to suit your preferences through the settings.

If you wish to access your calendar and contacts within the Mail app, click on the icons found at the bottom-left corner. Furthermore, you have the option to synchronize your calendar and contacts with external services like Google or iCloud, ensuring seamless integration of your information across platforms.

How to compose an email and attach files to an email

Composing an Email

To compose an email you have the option of utilizing either the integrated Mail app or the recently introduced Outlook app. Both applications provide the capability to craft and dispatch emails, complete with attachments, drawing from a variety of accounts and services. Here are the general steps for composing an email:

Using the Mail or Outlook App:

1. Initiate the process by launching either the Mail app or the Outlook app. You can access them by clicking on their respective icons located on your taskbar or by conducting a search for them within the Start menu.

2. Once the app is open, click on the New mail or New message button typically situated at the top-left corner of the app window.

3. In the ensuing window, proceed by entering the recipient's email address, formulating a subject line, and crafting the message body in the appropriate fields. Should you wish to include additional recipients, you can do so in the Cc (Carbon Copy) or Bcc (Blind Carbon Copy) fields, enabling you to send copies or blind copies to others.

4. When you've completed your email, you can proceed to send it by clicking on the Send button conveniently located at the top-right corner of the message window.

Attaching Files

Attaching files is a method for sharing various types of documents, photos, or files with your email contacts. You can employ either the integrated Mail app or the recently introduced Outlook app to append files to your emails. Below are the general steps for attaching files:

Using the Mail App:

1. To commence, open the Mail app, and access it by clicking on the envelope icon situated on your taskbar or by searching for it within the Start menu.

2. Once the Mail app is open, click on the New mail button located at the top-left corner of the app's interface.

3. In the ensuing window, input the recipient's email address, specify a subject line, and craft the message body as needed.

4. To attach a file, identify the Attach File button, usually positioned at the bottom of the message window. From there, you can select a file from your computer or your cloud locations, including OneDrive and SharePoint.

5. Once your email is composed and the desired file is attached, conclude the process by clicking on the Send button conveniently positioned at the top-right corner.

Using the New Outlook App:

1. Launch the new Outlook app, click on the calendar icon located on your taskbar, or by searching for it in the Start menu.

2. In the Outlook app, click on the New message button typically found at the top-left corner of the app's interface.

3. Begin by entering the recipient's email address, establishing a subject line, and formulating the message body according to your requirements.

4. To include an attachment, locate the Attach button situated at the top of the message window. You can then select a file from your computer or your cloud locations, such as OneDrive and SharePoint.

5. To send your email, click on the Send button located at the top-right corner of the message window.

How to read and reply to Emails

The integrated Mail app or the newly introduced Outlook app. Both of these applications offer the capability to manage and interact with emails originating from diverse accounts and services. Here are the general steps for reading and responding to emails:

Reading Emails:

1. To access and read an email, open either the Mail app or the Outlook app. You can initiate the app by clicking on its respective icon found on your taskbar or by conducting a search for it within the Start menu.

2. Within the app interface, select the specific email that you wish to read from the list of messages. Additionally, you can utilize swipe actions for expeditious email management. By swiping left or right on emails, you can swiftly execute actions like deletion, archiving, flagging, marking as read or unread, moving, or snoozing. Customizing these swipe actions can be done through the settings.

Replying to Emails:

1. To respond to an email within either the Mail app or the Outlook app, commence by opening the email that necessitates your reply.

2. Locate the Reply button, usually positioned at the top-right corner of the message window. Clicking this button will initiate the reply process.

3. Should you desire to reply to all recipients of the email or forward it to another individual, you can achieve this by clicking the arrow adjacent to the Reply button.

4. Proceed by typing your response within the message box. Once your reply is composed, finalize the process by clicking on the Send button, typically situated at the top-right corner of the message window.

5. If you wish to further enhance your email response, you can utilize various options found at the bottom or top of the message

window. These options include adding attachments, inserting pictures, formatting text, or incorporating emojis.

The Spam Folder

The spam folder serves as a repository for emails suspected to be unsolicited, unwanted, or potentially harmful. The nomenclature of this folder may vary depending on the specific email account and application you are using, often appearing under different names such as Junk, Bulk Mail, or Spam.

Accessing the spam folder can be accomplished through either the native Mail app or the newly introduced Outlook app. Both of these applications offer the functionality to view and manage emails across multiple accounts and services. Here are some general steps for accessing the spam folder:

Using the Mail App:

1. Initiate the Mail app by either clicking the envelope icon situated on your taskbar or by searching for it within the Start menu.
2. In the left pane of the Mail app, navigate to the More option to expand the list of folders. You may need to scroll down to locate it.
3. Locate and select the folder corresponding to your spam folder. For instance, if you are using a Yahoo account, it might be labeled as Bulk Mail. If you have an Outlook.com account, it may appear as a Junk E-Mail.
4. If you wish to streamline access to the spam folder, you can add it to your favorites by right-clicking on it and selecting Add to favorites. This action will place it within your standard list of folders for convenient access.

Using the New Outlook App:

1. Launch the new Outlook app, which can be accomplished by clicking on the calendar icon found on your taskbar or by conducting a search for it within the Start menu.
2. Within the left pane of the Outlook app, identify and click on the folder corresponding to your spam folder. For instance, a Gmail account might label it as Spam, while an Outlook.com account may use the term Junk Email.
3. Similar to the Mail app, you can streamline access to the spam folder in the Outlook app by adding it to your favorites. To do so, right-click on the folder and select Add to Favorites. This will incorporate it into your regular list of folders for easy access.

Creating folders and organizing Mail

Creating folders and subfolders in the Mail app allows you to organize your emails and keep your inbox tidy. Here's a step-by-step guide on how to create folders in Mail:

1. Open the Mail App: Launch the Mail app by clicking on the envelope icon on your taskbar or by searching for it in the Start menu.

2. Access the Folder Menu: In the Mail app, you will typically find the folder menu on the left-hand side of the window. If you don't see it, you can expand it by clicking on the three horizontal lines (hamburger menu) or a similar icon that represents the menu.

3. Add a New Folder:

- To create a new folder, locate and click on the + or New folder button within the folder menu. This action will initiate the folder creation process.
- A pop-up window or dialogue box will appear, prompting you to enter a name for your new folder. Type in a descriptive name that reflects the purpose or content of the folder.

- After naming the folder, confirm or save your choice. The new folder will now appear in the folder menu.

4. Organize Folders:
- To arrange your folders, you can use the drag-and-drop method. Click and hold the folder you want to move, and then drag it to the desired location within the folder menu.
- If you wish to create subfolders, you can do so by dragging a folder beneath another folder. This action will nest the folder as a subfolder under the parent folder.

5. Use and Manage Folders:
- To utilize your newly created folders, simply click on them to access or view their contents. You can move emails to specific folders by selecting the email and dragging it to the desired folder.
- You can also set up rules or filters to automatically route incoming emails to specific folders based on criteria you define, such as sender, subject, or keywords.

6. Additional Options:
- Depending on the specific version of the Mail app you are using, there may be additional options or settings related to folder management. Explore the app's settings or help resources for more information on customizing folder behavior.

Personalizing your Mail App

To access the Personalization settings in the Mail app, follow these steps:

1. Open the Mail App: launch the Mail app, click on the envelope icon on your taskbar, or search for it in the Start menu.

2. Access the Settings Button: Once the Mail app is open, you will typically find a navigation pane on the left side of the window. In this pane, locate and click on the Settings button. It's usually represented by a gearwheel or a similar icon and is positioned at the bottom of the navigation pane.

3. Open the Settings Flyout: Upon clicking the Settings button, a flyout menu will appear on the right side of the app window. This flyout menu contains various options and settings related to the Mail app's configuration.

4. Select Personalization: Within the Settings flyout, you'll see a list of categories or sections that pertain to different aspects of the Mail app's customization. Look for and click on the Personalization option. This section is where you can personalize and adjust various visual and behavioral settings within the app to suit your preferences.

5. Adjust Personalization Settings: Once you've entered the Personalization section, you'll have access to a range of settings that allow you to customize the app's appearance and behavior. These settings may include options related to themes, fonts, colors, background images, and more. Depending on your preferences and the specific version of the Mail app you are using, you can modify these settings to create a personalized email experience.

6. Save Changes (if applicable): After making any desired changes to the Personalization settings, ensure to save your modifications if required. The process for saving changes may vary depending on the specific settings you've adjusted.

Google Mail

Composing an email in Google Mail

To compose an email in Google Mail (Gmail) on a computer, you can follow these steps:

1. Access Gmail:

- Open your preferred web browser on your computer.
- In the web browser's address bar, enter mail.google.com and press Enter. Alternatively, you can search for Gmail in the Start menu and click on the web result.

2. Sign In or Create an Account:

- If you have a Google account, enter your email address and password to sign in.
- If you don't have a Google account, click on the Create account option to set up a new Google account by providing the required information.

3. Initiate Email Composition:

- After signing in, you'll be directed to your Gmail inbox.
- In the top-left corner of the Gmail interface, you'll find the Compose button. Click on this button to start composing a new email.

4. Enter Recipient(s):

- In the new message window, you'll see a To field where you can enter the recipient's email address. If you're sending the email to multiple recipients, you can also use the Cc (carbon copy) and Bcc (blind carbon copy) fields to include additional recipients.

5. Add a Subject:

- Beneath the recipient fields, there's a Subject field. Here, you should provide a concise and descriptive subject line for your email, summarizing the content or purpose of your message.

6. Compose Your Email:

- In the main message area of the email composition window, you can start typing your email message. You can use the text formatting toolbar located at the bottom of the message area to customize the font, text size, color, alignment, and style.
- Additionally, you can incorporate emojis, insert hyperlinks, attach files, embed images, or use other features provided by the icons located at the bottom of the message area.

7. Send or Save Your Email:

- Once your email is ready to be sent, click on the Send button located in the top-right corner of the message window.
- If you're not ready to send your email immediately, you have the option to save it as a draft, schedule it to be sent at a later time, or discard it using the respective icons adjacent to the Send button.

Google Mail settings

To access and adjust your Google Mail settings through a web browser:

1. Launch Your Web Browser:

- Open your preferred web browser on your computer.

2. Go to Gmail:

- In the browser's address bar, type mail.google.com and press Enter.
- Enter your Google account credentials to log in.

3. Access Settings:

- Once you're signed in to your Gmail account, locate and click on the gearwheel icon, typically found at the top-right corner of the Gmail interface.

4. Open Settings:

- From the dropdown menu, select See all settings. This action will take you to the Gmail Settings page.

5. Adjust Settings:
- On the Settings page, you'll find various tabs like General, Labels, Inbox, Accounts, Filters, and more.
- Each tab contains specific settings and preferences that you can customize according to your requirements.
- Click on the relevant tab to access the settings you want to modify.
- After making changes to your settings, don't forget to scroll to the bottom of the page and click Save Changes to apply your modifications.

How to Manage your email, schedule, and tasks using Microsoft Outlook

Step 1: Set Up Your Email Account in Outlook

Before you can start managing your email, schedule, and tasks in Microsoft Outlook, the first step is to set up your email account. This ensures that all your communications and calendar events are seamlessly integrated into the app. Here's how to get started:

1. **Open Outlook:** Begin by launching Microsoft Outlook on your computer. You can do this by searching for it in your Start menu or finding the Outlook icon on your desktop or taskbar.
2. **Go to the File Menu:** Once you have Outlook open, look at the top left corner of the window. You will see a menu called File. Click on it to open the file menu where all the main settings and options are located.

3. **Select "Add Account":** In the File menu, find and click on the Add Account option. This will open a new window where you can add your email account to Outlook.

4. **Enter Your Email Address and Password:** A prompt will appear asking for your email address. Type in your email address (e.g., example@gmail.com), then click Connect. Afterward, you will be prompted to enter your password for that email account. Make sure to input the correct information to continue.

5. **Follow the Setup Prompts:** After entering your email and password, Outlook will automatically detect your email service (such as Gmail, Yahoo, or Outlook.com). The program will then automatically configure most email services for you, so you won't need to manually set up any additional settings.

If everything is set up correctly, you'll see a message confirming that your email account has been successfully added.

6. **Complete the Setup:** Follow any additional prompts to finalize the setup. Outlook might ask you if you want to set up additional features or preferences, but for now, you can just proceed with the default settings. Once this is done, your email account will be fully set up and ready to use.

Step 2: Manage Your Email in Outlook

Outlook provides you with the tools you need to stay on top of your inbox. Here's how to effectively manage your email:

Reading and Replying to Emails

When you open Outlook, the first thing you will see is your Inbox, which contains all your incoming emails. The layout is clean and easy to navigate, ensuring you can quickly find and manage your messages.

To read an email, simply click on it. This will open the email in the reading pane or a new window, allowing you to view its content.

Once you've read an email, you can reply directly. You'll find options like Reply, Reply All, or Forward at the top of the email. Click Reply to respond only to the sender, Reply All to respond to everyone who received the email, or Forward to send the email to someone else.

Organizing Emails

Outlook helps you keep your inbox neat and organized by allowing you to create folders and use rules for automatic sorting.

- **Creating Folders:** You can create folders to store and categorize emails, making it easier to find messages later. Right-click on your Inbox, select New Folder, and give it a name. You can drag and drop emails into these folders to keep them organized by project, sender, or topic.

- **Using Rules:** Outlook also allows you to set up rules to automatically sort your emails. For instance, you can create a rule that moves all emails from a specific sender to a particular folder. To do this, go to Home > Rules > Manage Rules & Alerts. From there, you can create new rules to move, delete, or categorize incoming emails based on criteria like the sender, subject, or keywords.

Flagging and Categorizing Emails

Outlook also provides additional features like flagging and categorizing emails to help prioritize and stay organized.

- **Flagging Emails:** You can use flags to mark important emails. Right-click on an email, choose Follow Up, and select a due date. This will add a flag to the email, reminding you to follow up on it later.

- **Categorizing Emails:** Categorizing emails is a great way to keep track of different tasks or projects. Right-click on an email, select **Categorize** and choose a color. You can customize the categories to fit your needs, helping you quickly identify and prioritize emails.

Step 3: Manage Your Calendar and Schedule in Outlook

Microsoft Outlook's calendar feature is a tool that helps you stay organized by managing your appointments, meetings, and daily schedule. The calendar is easy to use, making it simple to add and track important events. Here's how you can manage your calendar effectively:

Accessing the Calendar

To begin, navigate to the Calendar tab by clicking on the calendar icon located at the bottom of the screen in Outlook. This will take you directly to the calendar view, where you can view all your scheduled events and appointments.

Create Appointments

Creating an appointment in Outlook is quick and straightforward. To add a new event, simply click on a time slot in your calendar, and an event window will pop up. Here, you can enter important details such as:

- **Title:** The name of the event (e.g., "Doctor's Appointment").
- **Location:** Where the event will take place.
- **Time:** Set the start and end times for the appointment.
- **Description:** Add any additional information or notes related to the event.

You can also set reminders to alert you ahead of time, so you don't forget about important appointments.

Set Recurring Events

For regular meetings or events that happen on a repeating basis, such as weekly team meetings or monthly reports, Outlook allows you to set recurring events. After entering the event details, select Recurrence in the event window. You can then choose how often the event should occur, whether it's daily, weekly, monthly, or yearly. This feature ensures that recurring events are automatically added to your calendar without having to manually enter them each time.

Schedule Meetings

Scheduling a meeting in Outlook is easy. In the Home tab, click on **New Meeting** to start. Enter the necessary details:

- **Attendees:** Add the emails of the people you want to invite by typing them in the To field.
- **Date and Time:** Set the start and end date and time for the meeting.
- **Attach Files:** You can also attach relevant files or documents that attendees will need for the meeting.

Once everything is set, click Send to send out the invitations. Outlook will automatically send a calendar invite to all attendees, and they will have the option to accept or decline.

Sharing Your Calendar

Sometimes, you may need to share your calendar with others so they can view your schedule or even make changes. To share your calendar, go to Home > Share Calendar. You will then be prompted to choose the calendar you want to share and specify the level of access (either view only or edit permissions). This is particularly useful for team collaborations or if you want your assistant or colleague to manage your schedule.

To share your calendar in Outlook on the web, follow these steps:

First, open Outlook on your web browser and go to your Calendar.

Next, right-click on the calendar you want to share and choose **Sharing and Permissions**.

Then, enter the email address of the person you want to share your calendar with.

In the dropdown menu, select Can view when I'm busy to allow the person to see your availability without sharing all the details.

Finally, click Share to send the invitation.

Verify Calendar Sharing Permissions in the New Outlook

To verify calendar sharing permissions in the new Outlook desktop app, start by clicking on the Calendar icon in the navigation bar on the left side of the screen.

Next, right-click on the calendar you wish to manage, located in the calendar list on the left.

From the context menu that appears, select Permissions.

In the Permissions pane, you will see a list of people who have access to your calendar.

Select the person whose permissions you'd like to adjust, or add a new one.

Using the dropdown menu, choose the appropriate permission level. The options may include:

- **Can view it when I'm busy** (only shows availability).
- **Can view titles and locations** (shows titles and locations of events).

- **Can view all details** (shows all event details).
- **Can edit** (allows changes to the calendar).

Once you select the permission level, the changes will be saved automatically.

Step 4: Manage Your Tasks in Outlook

Outlook isn't just about email and calendar management—it also includes a powerful task manager that helps you stay organized and on top of your to-do lists. With Outlook's task management features, you can create, organize, and track tasks, ensuring nothing slips through the cracks. Here's how you can manage your tasks in Outlook:

Access the Task Manager

First, click on the Tasks icon at the bottom of your Outlook screen. This will take you to the task management view, where you can create new tasks, view existing ones, and organize your to-do lists.

Create a New Task

To create a new task, go to the Home tab and click on New Task. A task creation window will pop up, where you can enter the task's details. You'll need to fill in:

- **Task Name:** The title or name of the task (e.g., "Finish report").
- **Due Date:** When you want the task to be completed.
- **Description:** Additional details or notes about the task.

You can also set reminders to ensure you don't forget about the task. For example, you can choose to be reminded 15 minutes before the due time.

Additionally, Outlook allows you to set priorities for your tasks (such as low, normal, or high) and attach files relevant to the task. This helps you keep everything connected in one place.

Organize Your Tasks

Organizing your tasks is key to staying efficient. Outlook allows you to use folders and categories to organize tasks based on priority or type. For example, you could create folders like "Work," "Personal," or "Urgent" to separate your tasks. You can also categorize tasks with specific colors to easily identify their type or priority.

Once you finish a task, you can mark it as Completed. This will move the task to your Completed folder and help you track your progress.

Set Up Recurring Tasks

For tasks that happen regularly, like weekly reports or daily check-ins, you can set them up to repeat automatically. After entering the task details, click on Recurrence in the task window. You'll be able to choose how often the task should repeat—daily, weekly, monthly, or on a custom schedule. This ensures that you never have to manually create the same task again.

View Your Task List

Outlook also offers a To-Do List view where you can see all of your tasks across various folders and categories in one place. This view helps you get an overall picture of your tasks, showing you what's due, what's pending, and what's completed. It's a great way to manage everything in one simple interface.

Step 5: Sync Your Devices with Outlook

One of the great advantages of using Microsoft Outlook is its ability to sync your email, calendar, and tasks across multiple devices. This ensures you can stay connected and organized no matter where you are, using your computer at home, on your phone during the commute, or using a tablet while traveling.

Syncing Outlook on Your Devices

Outlook is compatible with mobile apps, which makes it easy to access your emails, calendar, and tasks on the go. Using an iPhone, Android device, or tablet, syncing your Outlook account across your devices is simple and ensures you're always up to date with your information.

Mobile Setup

To get started, you'll need to download the Outlook app on your mobile device. Here's how:

1. **Download the Outlook App:**
   - For iPhone or iPad users, go to the App Store and search for Outlook.
   - For Android users, go to Google Play and search for Outlook.
2. **Install the App:** After finding the app, click on Install to download it to your device. The app will install in just a few seconds, and then you'll be ready to start syncing.
3. **Log In to Your Microsoft Account:** Once the app is installed, open it and log in using your Microsoft account (the same email address and password you use for Outlook on your computer).
4. **Access Your Email, Calendar, and Tasks:** Once logged in, your email, calendar, and tasks will be automatically synced with your mobile device. You can now read, respond to emails, add calendar events, and manage your tasks directly from the Outlook app, just like you would on your desktop or laptop.

Using Outlook on Your Tablet

The Outlook app is also available for tablets, so you can enjoy the same great features while on the move. Just download the app from your tablet's respective app store (iOS or Android), and once installed, log in with your Microsoft account. You'll be able to sync all your Outlook information—email, calendar, and tasks—on your tablet for easy access and management.

CONCLUSION

The Mail app offers a comprehensive email solution for many users, Nevertheless, it provides a convenient and integrated email experience that aligns with the modern design and features of Windows 11, making it a valuable tool for managing email communications efficiently. The Mail app allows users to access and read emails even when offline, ensuring that important messages are always available, regardless of the internet connection.

CHAPTER TEN

NETWORKING

Workgroups

A workgroup refers to a collection of personal computers linked within a local area network, all residing on the same subnet. These interconnected PCs collaborate in resource sharing, including access to printers and files. Each computer belonging to the workgroup can freely utilize shared resources offered by others and offer its resources for sharing. Within this network, all computers operate as equals, with no single computer exerting control or dominance over the others.

Here is how to access the workgroup:

1. Accessing Settings: To begin, click on the Windows icon in the taskbar or press the Windows key on your keyboard to open the Start Menu. From there, you can either click on the Settings gear icon in the left-hand panel or simply type Settings into the search bar and select it from the results.

2. Navigating to System Settings: In the Settings window, you'll see various categories on the left side. Scroll down and select System. This category encompasses all the settings related to your device's hardware, software, and network configurations.

3. About Section: Within the System category, you'll find a list of subcategories on the left. Scroll down and click on About. This section contains information about your device, including its specifications, Windows edition, and more.

4. Domain or Workgroup: In the About section, you should see a heading called Domain or Workgroup. This is where you can configure your device's network settings. Under Domain or Workgroup, you can click on the Change button to manage your device's network membership.

5. Changing Workgroup: Clicking on the Change button will open a new window where you can select either Domain or Workgroup. To join or create a workgroup, choose Workgroup and enter the name of the workgroup you want to join or create.

6. Restarting: After making changes to your workgroup settings, Windows may prompt you to restart your computer to apply these changes. It's important to do so for the new workgroup settings to take effect.

Chat Functionality

Chat is an innovative communication feature that empowers you to engage with your contacts through text, voice, or video calls. It harnesses the capabilities of Microsoft Teams, although it differs from the Teams application typically employed for professional or educational purposes. Chat is expressly designed for informal and personal interactions with your circle of friends and family.

Accessible directly from the taskbar, Chat provides seamless integration with your contacts from both Skype and Outlook. Beyond its core messaging functionality, Chat offers the versatility to create and participate in meetings, share files, and add some flair to your conversations with emojis, GIFs, and polls. With Chat, Windows 11 offers a user-friendly and efficient means to stay connected with your loved ones.

To set up the Chat app, follow these steps:

- Click on the Chat icon located in the taskbar, represented by a speech bubble with a camera icon.
- Click the Get Started button.
- Provide your first name, last name, and phone number. You can also synchronize your contacts from Skype and Outlook.
- Click the Let's Go button.

To utilize the Chat app, you can perform the following actions:

1. To initiate a text conversation, click the Chat icon in the taskbar, then click Chat once more. In the To: field, input the email or phone number of the individual you wish to contact and press Enter. You can then compose your message and send it. Additionally, you have the option to utilize text formatting, attach media, and incorporate emojis, GIFs, and polls into your chats.

2. To initiate a voice or video call, click the Chat icon in the taskbar, then select the Meet button. You can choose to create a new meeting or join an existing one. Furthermore, you can schedule a meeting for a later time. To establish a new meeting, enter a name for the meeting and click the Create button. Subsequently, you can invite participants by sending them a link or copying it to your clipboard. To join an existing meeting, enter the meeting code or link and click the Join button. You can also toggle your camera and microphone settings on or off before entering the meeting.

Transferring Files

To transfer files over a network you must share files or directories across a local area network (LAN), which typically includes interconnected computers within your home or workplace. Several methods are available for sharing files or folders over a network, including File Explorer, Command Prompt, or Robocopy. Here are the steps for each of these methods:

Using File Explorer:

- Right-click (or long-press) the file or folder you want to share, and then select Show more options > Give access to > Specific people.
- Choose a user from the network with whom you wish to share the file or folder, or select Everyone to grant access to all network users.
- Click the Share button.

To access the shared file or folder from another device, follow these steps:

- Open File Explorer on the remote device.
- Navigate to the Network section.
- Locate the name of the device that is sharing the file or folder.
- Double-click on the device name and provide the necessary credentials if prompted.
- You can then open or copy the shared file or folder as needed.

Using Command Prompt

For sharing a file or folder over a network using Command Prompt, follow these steps:

- Open Command Prompt with administrator privileges.
- Enter the following command: **net share name=path**, where name represents the name of the shared resource, and path denotes the full path of the file or folder you intend to share. For instance, you can input something like **net share photos=C:\Users\John\Pictures\Photos**.
- Press Enter. You should receive a confirmation message stating that the command was completed successfully.

To access the shared file or folder from another device, take these steps:

- Open File Explorer on the remote device.
- In the address bar, type **\\device-name\name**, replacing device-name with the name of the device that is sharing the file or folder, and name with the name of the shared resource. For example, you might enter **\\John-PC\photos**.
- You can then open or copy the shared file or folder as needed.

Guest Access

The guest access feature enables you to establish a temporary account for individuals who wish to use your computer without any impact on your files and settings. This guest account is intentionally restricted, with limited permissions that prevent the installation of software, alterations to system configurations, or access to your private data. The Guest access option proves invaluable when you need to share your computer with friends, family members, or visitors who merely require access for tasks like checking email, web browsing, or performing straightforward activities.

Here's a step-by-step explanation of how to perform these actions:

1. Open the Settings App:

- Begin by pressing the Windows Key (the key with the Windows logo) and the letter 'I' simultaneously on your keyboard. This key combination serves as a quick shortcut to open the Settings app.

2. Choose Accounts:

- After you've successfully opened the Settings app, you'll see various categories listed on the left sidebar. Locate and click on

Accounts. This section allows you to manage your user accounts and related settings.

3. Access Other users:

- Within the Accounts section, you'll find several options related to your account settings. Look for and select Other users. This section is where you can manage additional user accounts on your device.

4. Add an Account:

- Once you're in the Other Users section, you'll find an option to Add an Account. Click on it. This action initiates the process of adding a new user account to your computer.

5. Specify Sign-In Information:

- After clicking Add Account, you may be presented with different options. To add a local user account (one that is not tied to a Microsoft Account), click on I don't have this person's sign-in information. This choice is ideal for creating user accounts that are not linked to an email address or Microsoft services.

6. Create a User Account:

- Following the selection of I don't have this person's sign-in information, you'll be prompted to Add a user without a Microsoft Account. This option allows you to create a new user account with a username and password specific to your Windows 11 device, without requiring a Microsoft Account.

Domains

Domains serve as a means to effectively organize and oversee a network comprising interconnected computers within the same local area network (LAN). These domains are under the administration of one or more servers, referred to as domain controllers, which possess the authority to establish regulations and policies for all members within the domain. A domain can encompass a considerable number of computers, users, and resources, encompassing items like printers, files, and applications.

Domains prove particularly advantageous for large-scale organizations, such as businesses, educational institutions, or government entities that require centralized control and security for their network devices. By integrating a computer into a domain, numerous benefits can be realized, including:

1. Single Sign-On: Users gain the ability to log in to any computer within the domain using the same set of credentials, eliminating the need for multiple usernames and passwords. Additionally, access to shared resources within the domain becomes seamless, as additional authentication isn't required.

2. Group Policies: Domain administrators can implement settings and restrictions across all or select computers within the domain. This entails enforcing security protocols, deploying software updates, or customizing the appearance of the desktop environment.

3. Roaming Profiles: Users benefit from a consistent desktop environment, even when working across various computers within the domain. Personal files and settings are stored on a server and synchronized with the local computer during login and logout processes.

4. Active Directory: Domain controllers utilize Active Directory to maintain a comprehensive database of information about domain objects, such as users, computers, groups, and permissions. Active Directory offers a hierarchical structure for the systematic organization and management of these domain objects, simplifying administrative tasks and enhancing network efficiency.

To enable domain joining in Windows 11, follow these steps:

1. Navigate to System and Security, and then select System.
2. In the System window, locate the section titled Computer name, domain, and workgroup settings.
3. Click on Change settings.
4. In the System Properties window, go to the Computer Name tab.
5. Click the Change button.
6. Under the Member of the section, select Domain.
7. Enter the name of the domain that you want this computer to join.
8. Click OK to confirm your choice.

IP Addresses and Configuration

An IP address serves as a distinct marker that enables devices to engage in communication across a network. These addresses can fall into one of two categories: static or dynamic, contingent on how they are allocated and configured.

A static IP address remains constant and is often manually established by either the user or a network administrator. Conversely, a dynamic IP address is subject to automatic alterations and is typically assigned by a DHCP (Dynamic Host Configuration Protocol) server.

Setting up a static IP address on your computer can be advantageous for various reasons. For instance, it allows you to facilitate remote access to your computer, share files and printers seamlessly with other devices, or configure port forwarding to support specific applications.

Using setting

Utilizing the Settings App: Employing the Settings app proves to be the simplest and most direct approach for configuring a static IP address on Windows 11. Within this app, you can modify the IP assignment settings for both your Ethernet and Wi-Fi connections. To successfully set up a static IP address, it is essential to possess knowledge of your existing IP address, subnet mask, default gateway, and DNS server addresses, as you will be adjusting these values to static configurations.

Here's how you can do it:

1. To begin, access the Windows Settings by either pressing Windows Key + I on your keyboard or searching for settings in the Start menu and clicking on the app icon. Once the Settings app is open, proceed to the next step.

2. Within the Settings, navigate to the Network & Internet section, which can be found in the sidebar on the left.

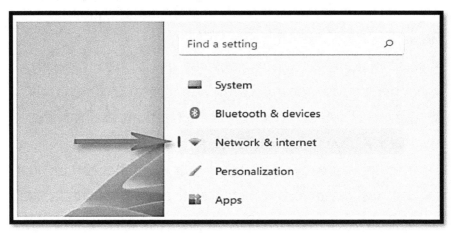

3. In the Network & Internet settings, you will find your primary Internet connection listed near the top of the window. Click on

Properties located next to the name of your network connection.

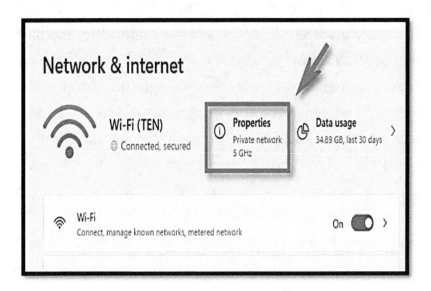

4. On the network connection properties page, scroll down until you reach the information section at the bottom. Here, you will find your local IP address in IPv4 format, typically displayed as something like 192.168.1.90. Additionally, your IPv6 address will be listed just above your IPv4 address.

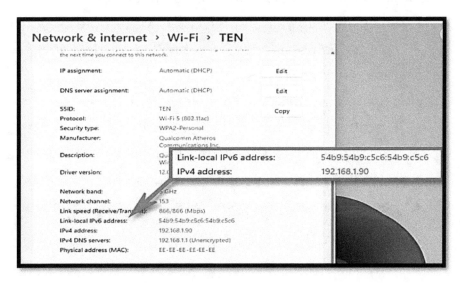

Using command prompt

Utilizing Command Prompt: While this approach may be more technically involved, it offers a faster method to establish a static IP address in Windows 11. With Command Prompt, you can execute a single command to create a local account with a static IP address configuration. However, it is imperative to have the following details readily available: the network adapter's name, along with the preferred IP address, subnet mask, default gateway, and DNS server addresses. You can conveniently locate this information on the Network Connections page within the Control Panel.

Configuring IP from Command Prompt can be a technical but efficient process. Here's a detailed guide on how to set a static TCP/IP configuration:

1. Access the Command Prompt:

- Initiate the Start menu and input cmd into the search box.
- Right-click on Command Prompt and choose Run as administrator.

2. Check Your Current Network Configuration:

- Enter ipconfig /all and hit Enter. Make note of your network adapter name, IP address, subnet mask, default gateway, and DNS server addresses.

3. Set a Static IP Address for Your Network Adapter:

- Execute netsh interface ipv4 set address name=adapter name static ip_address subnet_mask default_gateway to assign a static IP address to your network adapter.
- Replace the adapter name with your specific network adapter name (e.g., Wi-Fi).

- Replace ip_address, subnet_mask, and default_gateway with your preferred values (e.g., 192.168.1.100, 255.255.255.0, and 192.168.1.1).

4. Configure a Static DNS Server Address:
- Utilize netsh interface ipv4 set dns name=adapter name static dns_server_address to establish a static DNS server address for your network adapter.
- Replace the adapter name with your network adapter's name (e.g., Wi-Fi).
- Replace dns_server_address with your desired DNS server value (e.g., 8.8.8.8).

5. Clear the DNS Cache:
- Enter ipconfig /flushdns and press Enter to purge the DNS cache.

Dynamic and Static IP addresses

A dynamic IP address is allocated by a DHCP server, typically your router, and has the potential to change over time. On the other hand, a static IP address remains fixed unless you manually modify it. Static IP addresses are useful for specific tasks such as configuring printers, facilitating file sharing, or enabling port forwarding.

Windows 11, Microsoft's latest operating system, offers a range of enhancements and features, including the ability to customize your IP address settings. You have the flexibility to select either a dynamic or static IP address depending on your network requirements and personal preferences.

For those opting for a dynamic IP address, these steps can be followed:

1. Access Settings
2. Click on Network & Internet.
3. Choose the Wi-Fi or Ethernet tab, based on your current connection type.
4. Select your active network connection.
5. Under the IP settings section, click the Edit button.
6. From the drop-down menu, select the Automatic (DHCP) option.
7. Turn on the IPv4 toggle switch.
8. Lastly, click the Save button to confirm the changes.

DHCP

DHCP, which stands for Dynamic Host Configuration Protocol, is a networking protocol designed to streamline the process of assigning IP addresses and other network settings to devices within a network. This protocol enables devices to automatically acquire their IP addresses and related configurations from a DHCP server. Typically, a DHCP server is a router or a computer that maintains a pool of available IP addresses and allocates them to devices upon request. DHCP eliminates the need for manual IP configuration, making it simpler to connect devices to a network.

To enable DHCP or modify other TCP/IP settings on Windows 11, you can utilize either the Settings app or the Control Panel. Below are the step-by-step instructions for both methods:

Using the Settings App:
1. Launch the Settings app.
2. Select Network & Internet from the options.
3. Choose the appropriate tab, either Wi-Fi or Ethernet, depending on your current connection type.
4. Click on the active network connection.

5. Within the IP settings section, click the Edit button.

6. From the drop-down menu, choose Automatic (DHCP).

7. Activate the IPv4 toggle switch.

8. Confirm your changes by clicking the Save button.

Using the Control Panel:

1. Open the Start menu and enter Control Panel into the search box.

2. Click on Control Panel when it appears in the search results.

3. In the upper right-hand corner, you'll see View By. Click on it and select Large Icons.

4. Locate and click on Network and Sharing Center.

5. In the center of the new window, find the Network section and click on Ethernet0 connections.

6. A small window will appear; select the Properties button located near the bottom of the window.

7. In the new Properties window, choose Internet Protocol Version 4 (TCP/IPv4).

8. While Internet Protocol Version 4 is highlighted, select Properties to access another window.

9. Check the boxes labeled Obtain an IP address automatically and Obtain DNS server address automatically.

10. Save your changes by clicking OK.

Wireless Setup

To set up a wireless network you'll require a few essential components: a broadband Internet connection, a modem, a wireless router, and a wireless network adapter for your PC (although most laptops and tablets already have this built-in). Here's a step-by-step guide to help you with the wireless network setup:

1. Connect Your Modem:

- Link your modem to your Internet service provider (ISP) via a phone jack or a cable jack, depending on your type of connection.

2. Connect Your Wireless Router:

- Use an Ethernet cable to connect your wireless router to your modem. Insert one end of the cable into the WAN (Wide Area Network) port on the router and the other end into the LAN (Local Area Network) port on the modem.

3. Power On Router and Modem:

- Plug in and switch on your router and modem. Allow them some time to initialize and establish a connection. This process may take a few minutes.

4. Configure Wireless Settings on Your PC:

- On your PC, access the Taskbar and click on the Network icon, or press Windows+i to open the Settings app and then click on Network & Internet.

5. Enable Wi-Fi:

- Click the button next to the Wi-Fi icon in the top-right corner to activate Wi-Fi on your PC.

6. Select Your Wireless Network:

- From the list of available networks, choose the wireless network you wish to connect to. If your network isn't visible, you may need to manually input its name (SSID) by clicking Add Network at the bottom of the list.

7. Enter Network Security Key:

- If prompted, enter the network security key (password) for your wireless network and click Next. You can also select the Connect automatically option if you want your PC to remember this network and connect to it automatically in the future.

202

8. Choose Network Discoverability:

- Determine whether you want your device to be discoverable on the network. This choice will impact how other devices can access your PC and its resources, such as files and printers.

Setting up UHM Wireless on Windows 11 at UH-Manoa Campus

If you're looking to connect to the UHM (University of Hawaii at Manoa) wireless network on your Windows 11 computer while on the UH-Manoa campus, follow these step-by-step instructions:

1. Access Settings menu

- Press the Windows key and the I key simultaneously to open the Settings menu.

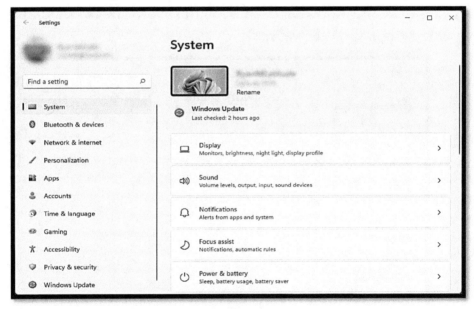

2. Navigate to Network & Internet:

- Within the Settings menu, select Network & Internet from the options on the left-hand side.

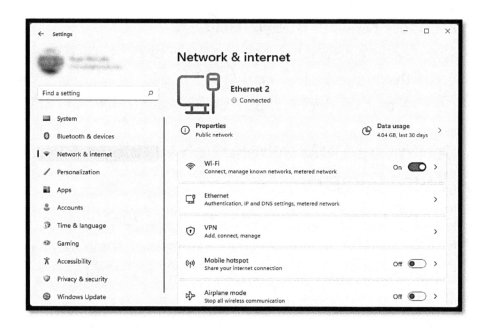

3. Choose Wi-Fi Settings:

- On the right-hand side of the Network & internet settings window, click on Wi-Fi.

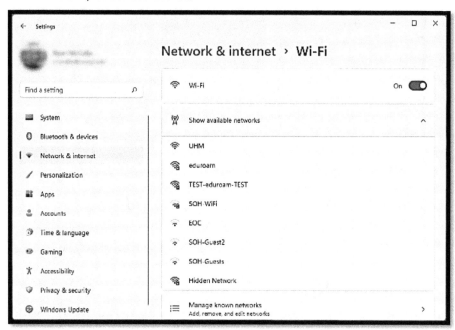

4. View Available Networks:

- In the Wi-Fi settings, select Show available networks. This action will display a list of all available wireless networks in your vicinity.

5. Select UHM Network:

- Locate UHM from the list of available networks and click on it to choose it as your network.

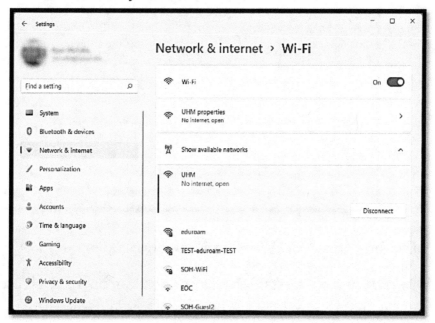

6. Automatic Connection (Optional):

- If you prefer to connect automatically to the UHM network in the future, check the Connect automatically option.

7. Connect to UHM:

- Click the Connect button. Windows will initiate the connection process and show you its progress as it attempts to connect to the UHM wireless network.

8. Confirm Connection:

- To verify that you've successfully connected to the UHM network, look at the wireless icon in the bottom-right corner of your screen. UHM should be listed as Connected, open.

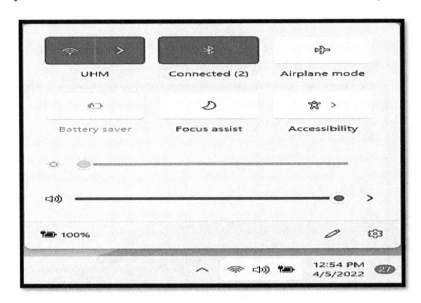

9.Log Into the UHM Wireless Network:

- Once you've established a connection, open a web browser like Edge, Chrome, or Mozilla Firefox. You'll need to log in to the wireless network using the authentication page provided by UHM.

CONCLUSION

A workgroup represents a decentralized network structure where individual computers within a local area network (LAN) collaborate on a peer-to-peer basis. They freely share resources like printers and files without any centralized control. Workgroups are ideal for small-scale networks where simplicity and ease of resource sharing are prioritized. On the other hand, domains offer a more organized and controlled approach to network management. They are overseen by domain controllers, typically servers, which enforce regulations and policies across a network. Domains are particularly beneficial for larger networks, as they provide centralized administration, user authentication, and resource management.

IP addresses play a pivotal role in network communication by providing a unique identifier to each device connected to the network. Dynamic IP addresses are assigned by a DHCP server and can change over time, making them suitable for most devices in a network. Static

IP addresses, on the other hand, remain fixed and are useful for specific tasks that require consistent addressing, such as configuring printers or enabling port forwarding.

In summary, workgroups, domains, and IP addresses are fundamental components of network architecture, each serving distinct purposes in managing and facilitating communication within local area networks. The choice between these components depends on the scale and requirements of the network, with workgroups offering simplicity, domains providing centralized control, and IP addresses ensuring seamless device identification and communication.

CHAPTER ELEVEN

HAVING FUN WITH WINDOWS 11

Taking Photos and Videos

Capturing and enhancing photos and videos in Windows 11 is a breeze, thanks to the user-friendly Camera app, the revamped Photos app, and the powerful Microsoft Clipchamp app for video editing.

Camera App:
- You can effortlessly snap photos and record videos using your PC's built-in webcam or an external camera.
- Access the Camera app by clicking on Start > Camera or simply by searching for a camera in the search box.
- The Camera app boasts a plethora of adjustable settings and modes, such as timers, flash, HDR, panorama, and more.
- You have the flexibility to switch between front and rear cameras if your device supports both.
- Taking a photo is as simple as clicking the camera icon or hitting the spacebar while recording a video involves clicking the video icon or pressing Ctrl+R. To stop recording, click the stop icon or press Ctrl+R once more.
- Your photos and videos are conveniently stored in the Pictures folder on your PC.

Photos App:
- As the default app for viewing, organizing, and editing media files the Photos app features an intuitive new design for seamless navigation.

- You can easily locate specific photos or videos using keywords, dates, locations, or people through the search function.
- The Photos app seamlessly integrates with cloud storage services like OneDrive and iCloud, enabling you to access your cloud-stored media from any device.
- To edit a photo, select it and click Edit image or press Ctrl+E. You can make various adjustments, including cropping, rotating, filtering, and markup. The app also offers AI-driven enhancements like background blur.
- For video editing, you'll need the Microsoft Clipchamp app.

Microsoft Clipchamp App:
- Clipchamp is an advanced AI-powered video editor and creation tool designed specifically for Windows 11.
- It simplifies the video editing process, eliminating the need for extensive expertise or expensive software.
- Clipchamp's features include multitrack editing, screen recording, access to a stock library, filters, effects, customizable brand kit designs, and more.
- The AI auto-assembly feature provides helpful editing suggestions based on your video content.
- To use Clipchamp, log in with your Microsoft account and select a subscription plan. You can start with the free plan, which supports video exports up to 1080p resolution, or upgrade to the essentials plan for additional features and up to 4K resolution.

Viewing your Photos and Videos

Using the Photos App

To seamlessly browse and enjoy your collection of photos and videos using the Photos app, follow these straightforward steps:

1. Open the Photos App:

- Launch the Photos app by selecting Start > Photos. Alternatively, you can quickly access it by typing photos into the search box on the taskbar and selecting the Photos app from the search results.

2. View Your Media Files:

- Upon opening, the Photos app will automatically present the photos and videos stored in your Pictures folder on your PC and those in your OneDrive account.
- If you have media in other folders, you can expand your content by selecting Folders in the left navigation bar and then clicking Add a folder.

3. View Photos and Videos:

- To view a specific photo or video, simply click on it. You can also navigate through your media files using the arrow keys on your keyboard.
- Zoom in or out of a photo using the mouse wheel, or press F11 to enter full-screen mode.

4. Utilize Collections:

- Organize your media by date, location, or people using the Collections feature in the Photos app.
- Access Collections by clicking on the Collections icon found in the left navigation bar.
- Create custom collections by selecting Create Collection in the top-right corner of the screen and adding photos and videos to it.

5. Enjoy Slideshows:

- If you want to enjoy your photos and videos as a dynamic slideshow, utilize the Slideshow feature within the Photos app.
- Access Slideshow by clicking on the Slideshow icon located in the top-right corner of the screen.
- Customize your slideshow settings, such as duration, transition effects, background music, and themes, by clicking on the Settings icon next to the Slideshow icon.

Viewing Details

To view the details of your photos and videos using the Photos app follow these steps:

1. Open the Photos App:
- Click on the Start button, and then select Photos from the menu.
- Type photos into the search box located on the taskbar, and then choose the Photos app from the search results.

2. View Your Media Files:
- The Photos app will automatically present the photos and videos stored in your Pictures folder on your PC and those in your OneDrive account.
- If you have media in other folders, you can expand your content by selecting Folders in the left navigation bar and then clicking Add a folder.

3. Access Photo and Video Details:
- For more information about a photo or video, including its name, date, size, resolution, and location, right-click on the item and choose Properties.

- To delve into detailed metadata such as camera model, aperture, shutter speed, ISO, and more, click on the Info icon located in the top-right corner of the screen.

Editing Pictures

To enhance and modify your photos follow these steps for more detailed editing options:

1. Access the Editing Tools:

- Begin by launching the Photos app on your computer.

2. Choose the Edit & Create Option:

- At the top of the screen, you'll find the Edit & Create button. Click on it to access the editing features.

3. Select Your Editing Category:

- Within the Edit & Create menu, you'll find several editing categories. Choose the one that suits your editing needs:

a. Crop & Rotate:

- Select this option if you want to adjust the composition of your photo by cropping it to remove unwanted elements or straightening it to the correct angles.

b. Filters:

- Opt for this option if you want to apply artistic filters to your photo. Filters can dramatically change the overall look and mood of your image.

c. Adjustments:

- Choose this category to fine-tune various aspects of your photo, including:
- **Light**: Adjust brightness, contrast, and exposure to control the overall lighting of your image.

- **Color**: Modify color saturation, temperature, and tint to achieve the desired color balance.
- **Clarity**: Enhance or soften details to make your photo sharper or give it a softer appearance.
- **Red-Eye Removal:** This tool helps you eliminate the red-eye effect often caused by camera flashes in portraits.

4. Edit Your Photo:
- After selecting your desired editing category, use the available tools and sliders to make adjustments. You can interactively manipulate these settings until you achieve the desired effect.

5. Apply Changes:
- Once you've finished editing your photo, look for an option to apply or save your changes. This may vary depending on the specific editing tool you've used.

6. Save Your Edited Photo:
- Don't forget to save your edited photo once you're satisfied with the results. Typically, there will be an option to save or overwrite the original photo with the edited version.

Create an Album

Creating an album allows you to organize and manage your photos and videos.

1. Launch the Photos App:
- Click the Start button, then choose Photos
- Quickly access it by typing photos into the search box on the taskbar, and then selecting the Photos app from the search results.

2. Access the Albums Section:

- In the Photos app, locate and click on the Albums option, typically found in the left navigation pane.

3. Create a New Album:

- Once you are within the Albums section, look for and select the Create new album option. This option is typically located at the top-right corner of the screen.

4. Select Photos for Your Album:

- Now, you can choose the photos you want to include in your album from your photo library. You can also use the search box to find specific photos by keywords, dates, locations, or people.

5. Edit Album Details (Optional):

- If desired, you can further customize your album. This includes editing the title of the photo album or changing the cover photo. To do this, simply click on the Edit icon next to the respective fields and make your adjustments.

6. Save Your Album:

- Once you're satisfied with your selections and any edits you've made, click on the Create button. This action will save your newly created album.

Creating a Slideshow

Creating a slideshow is a versatile process that can be accomplished using different built-in features and apps. Below, you'll find various methods to create slideshows:

Method 1: Using the Photos App

1. Open the Photos App:

- Click on the Start button, then select Photos from the list of available apps.

- Type photos into the search box located on the taskbar. From the search results, click on the Photos app to launch it swiftly.

2. Select Photos for Your Slideshow:
- Choose the photos from your library that you wish to include in your slideshow. You can also utilize the search box to locate specific photos by keywords, dates, locations, or people.

3. Create a New Video Project:
- Click on New at the top of your screen, then select New video project from the drop-down menu.

4. Edit Your Slideshow Presentation:
- Customize your slideshow by adding transitions, effects, text, stickers, and more to your slides. You can also incorporate music either from your PC or the Photos app's library.

5. Finalize Your Slideshow Video:
- After editing, click on Finish video at the top of your screen. Choose the video quality and assign a file name for your slideshow video.

6. Export or Share Your Slideshow:
- To save your slideshow video, click on Export or Share. You can store it on your PC or share it online.

Method 2: Using the Slideshow Feature

1. Access the Slideshow Feature:
- Right-click on a photo in your collection and select Slideshow from the context menu.

2. Customize Slideshow Settings:
- Click on the Settings icon at the top-right corner of the screen to configure your slideshow settings. You can adjust the duration for each photo, choose transition effects, set background music, and apply themes.

3. Save Your Settings:

- After configuring your preferences, click Save to apply the changes.

Method 3: Using Video Editor

1. Open Video Editor:
- Launch Video Editor by selecting Start > Video Editor. Alternatively, you can access it by typing video editor into the search box on the taskbar and selecting Video Editor from the results.

2. Create a New Video Project:
- Start a new video project and provide it with a name.

3. Add Media to Your Project:
- Include photos and videos from your PC or Video Editor's library in your storyboard or timeline. You can also utilize the screen recorder or webcam features if needed.

4. Edit Your Slideshow Presentation:
- Customize your slideshow by trimming, splitting, rotating, resizing, or applying various effects to your clips. You can also add transitions, filters, text, stickers, audio, and more to your slides.

5. Finalize Your Slideshow Video:
- Once your editing is complete, click on Finish Video at the top of your screen. Choose the video quality and specify a file name for your slideshow video.

6. Export or Share Your Slideshow:
- To save your slideshow video, click on Export or Share. You can store it on your PC or share it online.

Automatic Video

Automatic video is a feature that allows you to create a video from your photos and videos using the Photos app. You can use automatic video to make quick and easy videos for various occasions, such as birthdays, holidays, or family events. You can also customize your automatic video with music, transitions, effects, and more.

1. Launch the Photos App:

- Open the Photos app on your system.

2. Start a New Auto Video:

- On the Photos home screen, locate and click the New icon.

3. Select Your Photos:

- Choose Auto Video from the options presented and mark the checkboxes next to the photos you wish to include in your video.

4. Initiate Video Creation:

- Click Create to begin the automatic video generation process.

5. Name Your Video:

- Assign a suitable name to your video file in the prompt that appears, then click OK.

6. Preview Your Video:

- Your automatic video will be swiftly created, and you'll be presented with a preview window. This preview includes animation, background music, and stylized text derived from your video's title.

7. Customize as Desired:

- Should the initial video not meet your expectations, simply click Remix for me. The app's Artificial Intelligence will promptly generate another version with a fresh theme and different music. Feel free to continue remixing until your video aligns with your preferences.

8. Finish and Save Your Video:

- Once satisfied, click Finish Video. Opt for your preferred resolution (1080p is recommended), then click Export to save and enjoy your automatically created video.

Editing Videos

Clipchamp is a versatile video editor crafted by Microsoft for Windows. To access the full spectrum of Clipchamp's capabilities, consider upgrading to a premium subscription.

If you don't already have Clipchamp on your device, obtain it from the Microsoft Store and install it on your PC.

1. Initiate Video Creation:

- Choose either Create a video or Record something to begin crafting a video from scratch. Your selection doesn't matter, as you can incorporate both elements within the same project.

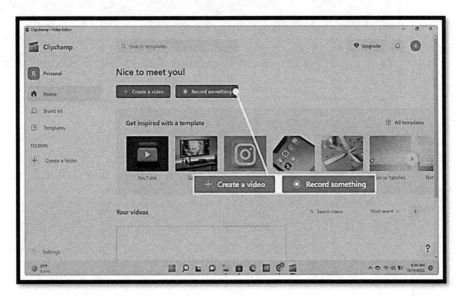

2. Exploring Record & Create (If Applicable):

- If you opt for Record Something, a new project in the Record & create tab will open. Here, you can record your screen, camera, or a combination of both. Additionally, there's a text-to-speech option.

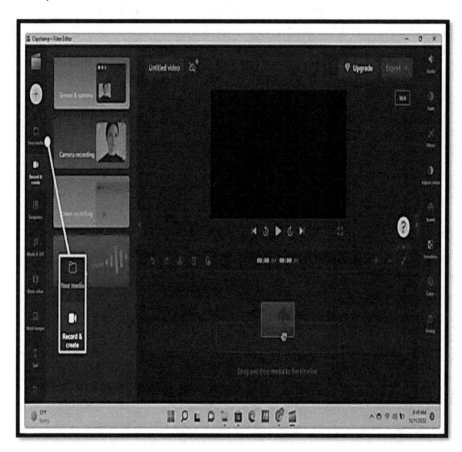

3. Media Management (If Applicable):

- For those who select Create a Video, the Your Media tab in a new project opens. You can easily switch between tabs at any point. To populate your project, click the Plus sign (+) to add videos, audio tracks, and images from your computer.

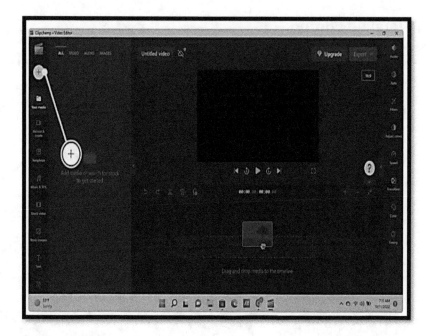

4. Accessing Clipchamp Features:

- Locate the Clipchamp icon in the upper-left corner, allowing you to save your work, initiate a new project, or return to the Home screen.

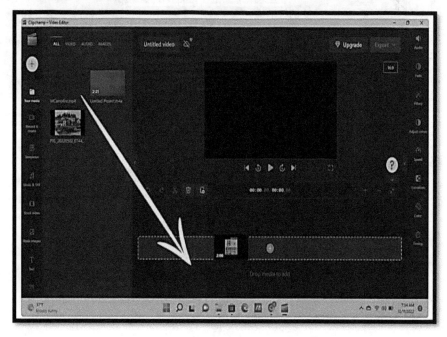

5. Timeline Editing:

- Once your media is uploaded, drag and drop the files into the timeline. As you add files, they will appear on separate tracks, permitting independent editing and repositioning. Right-click an element in the timeline for various options, or employ the toolbars adjacent to the preview window for focused editing.

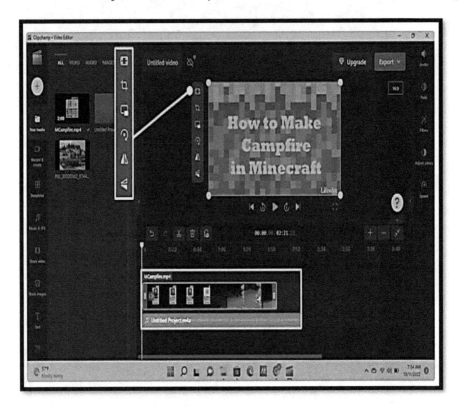

6. Exploring Templates and Resources:

- On the left-hand side, navigate to the Templates tab to discover built-in templates suited for diverse social media platforms. You'll also find integrated sound effects, music, stock images, and more. Click the downward arrow to reveal all the options.

7. Timeline Manipulation:

- To cut video and audio tracks, select an element, move the playback arrow to your desired location, and then utilize the Snip tool (depicted as scissors) beneath the preview window. You can also delete and duplicate tracks. To select multiple tracks, press and hold Shift while making your selection.

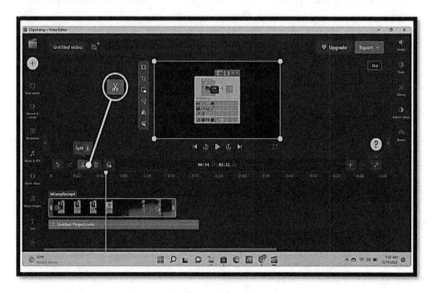

8. Track-Specific Options:

- The toolbar on the right side adapts according to your selection. For instance, when you select a video or image, you can access Transitions. Position your cursor between two elements in the same track, click the plus (+) icon, and pick a transition. Audio tracks offer options for fading in and out.

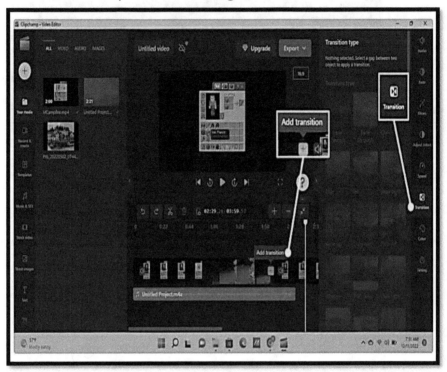

9. Naming Your Project:

- Before saving and exporting your video, assign it a distinctive title. Click the Untitled video above the preview window to rename your project.

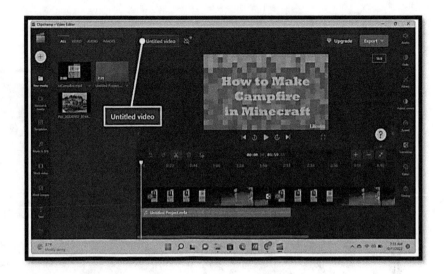

10. Exporting Your Video:

- Select Export, then specify the output quality to commence video creation. Note that a Clipchamp premium subscription is necessary for HD videos.

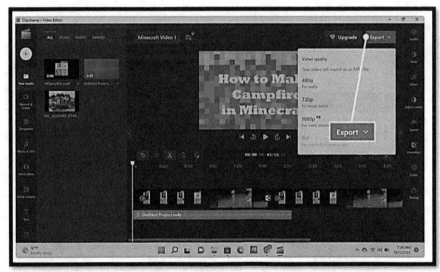

11. Monitor Progress:

- Observe your video being generated in real-time. Opt for one of the sharing alternatives to post your video on social media. Alternatively, click Keep Editing to return to your work on another project while your video continues exporting in the background.

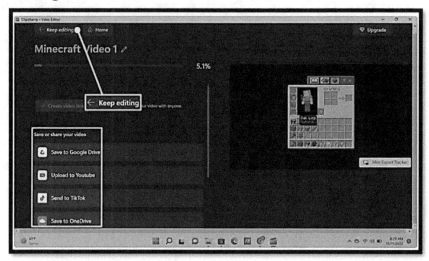

12. Accessing Your Video:

- Once your video is ready, select Open File in the pop-up notification to view it. Alternatively, choose Create video link to share it with your desired audience.

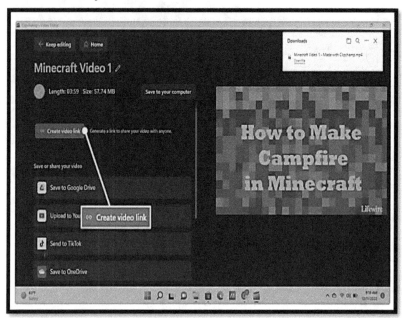

How to Edit Videos Using the Photos App

The Windows Photos app boasts an integrated video editor, which, while not as feature-rich as Clipchamp, can be an excellent choice for straightforward projects. Here's how to use it:

1. Launch the Photos App:

- Access the Start Menu and open the Photos app.

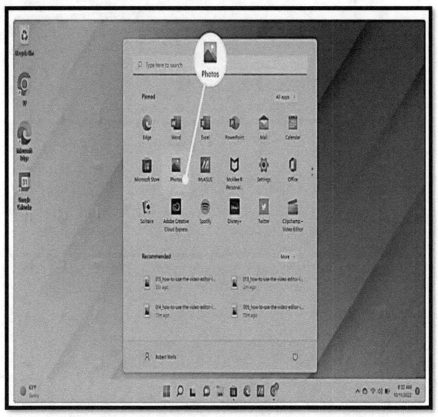

2. Enter Video Editor:

- Within the Photos app, select Video Editor.

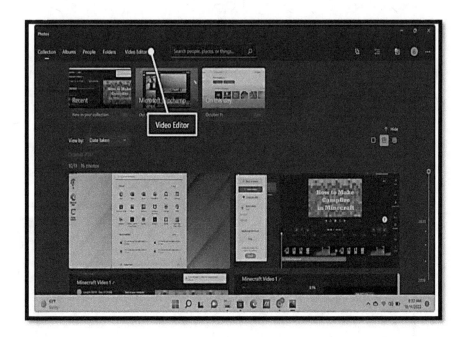

3. Start a New Video Project:

- Click New Video Project and assign a name to your video project. If you require additional editing capabilities, you might spot a link to Clipchamp in the Microsoft Store.

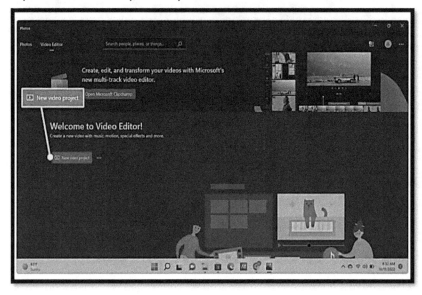

4. Add Media Files:

- Select Add + to incorporate video or image files into your project.

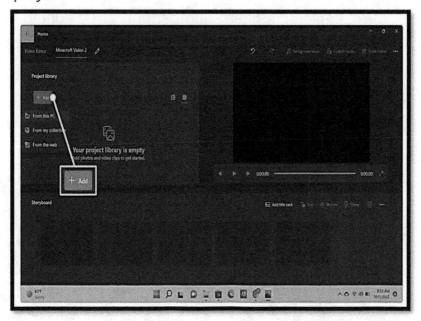

5. Arrange Your Media:

- Click and drag the media you've uploaded onto the storyboard. The storyboard allows you to sequence your content as desired.

6. Apply Edits:

- Utilize the toolbar situated under the preview window to insert text, implement filters, and perform other editing actions. You can rearrange the order of items on the storyboard by simply clicking and dragging them.

7. Finish Your Video:

- Once you're content with your edits, click Finish Video located in the upper-right corner.

Facial Recognition

Facial recognition is a cutting-edge feature that grants you access to your device by utilizing your facial features rather than traditional methods like passwords, PINs, or fingerprints. This technology employs specialized hardware such as an infrared or Intel RealSense camera to meticulously scan and validate your facial characteristics, offering a heightened level of security and convenience. This remarkable capability is seamlessly integrated into the Windows Hello suite, which encompasses various advanced biometric authentication methods.

Setting Up Facial Login: A Step-by-Step Guide

1. Access Settings: Begin by opening the Windows 11 Settings menu and select Accounts from the sidebar.

2. Choose Sign-in Options: In the Accounts section, click on Sign-in options.

3. Enable Facial Recognition: Locate Facial Recognition (Windows Hello) and click Set up.

4. Start the Setup: A Windows Hello setup window will appear. Click Get Started. If you already have a PIN set up, you will be prompted to enter it at this point.

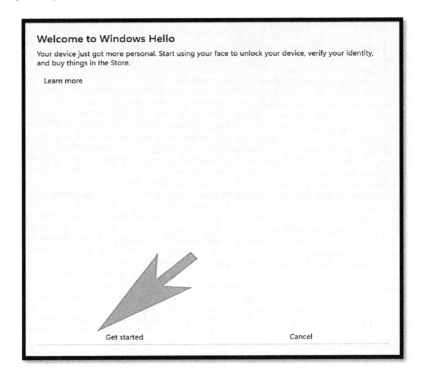

5. Face Scanning: Position yourself in front of your device's webcam. You will observe it scanning your face. If you haven't configured a PIN yet, Windows 11 will insist on setting one up.

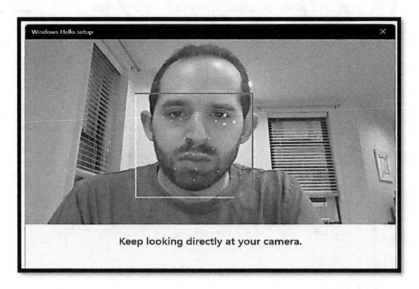

6. Completion: Once the scanning is complete, click Close to conclude the setup. If you wish to improve the recognition by capturing additional facial data (e.g., with or without glasses), click Improve Recognition.

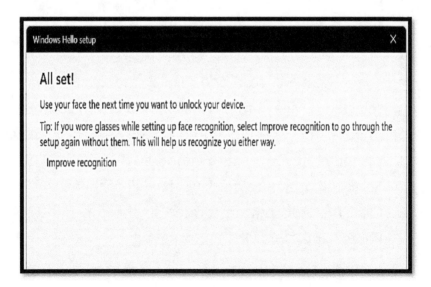

Upload Images to the Photos App

To import images from the Photos app follow these steps:

1. Open the Photos app on your computer.
2. Click on the Import menu within the Photos app.
3. Select the device from which you want to import photos. This could be your phone, camera, USB flash drive, SD card, or any other storage device you've connected to your computer.

4. The system will scan and display the available images on the selected device. It might take a moment to complete this scan.
5. Choose the specific photos you wish to transfer to your computer. If you want to import all the photos, you can use the Select All option to quickly select all of them.
6. Click the Add button located in the top-right corner of the Photos app.

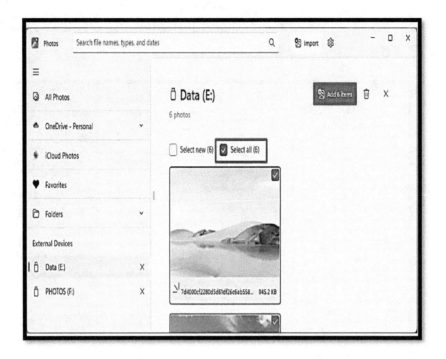

7. Next, click the Change button to specify the location and folder where you want to import the selected photos.

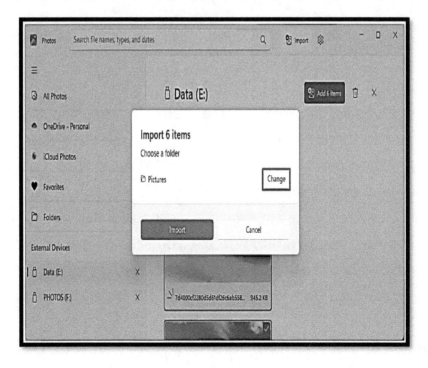

8. You can choose an existing location or create a new folder to group the imported files.

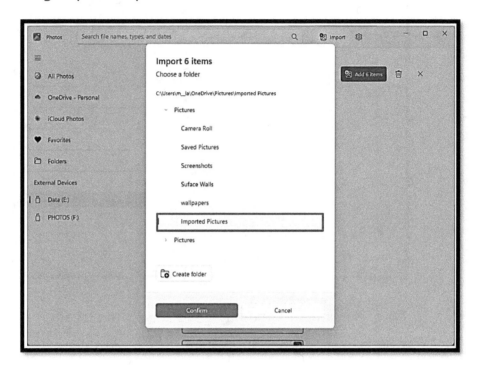

9. After selecting the import location, click the Confirm button to confirm your choice.

10. Finally, click the Import button to start the import process.

Once you've completed these steps, the selected photos will be imported to the destination folder you specified. It's important to note that this process will copy the image files to your computer while leaving the original images on the source storage device.

To complete the transfer, you may need to connect your phone to your computer. On an Android device, you can connect your phone using a USB cable, open the phone's settings, navigate to Connected devices, select USB, and choose the File Transfer option under the Use USB section.

Importing Photos from File Explorer on Windows 11:

To import your photos through File Explorer, use the following steps:

1. Open File Explorer on your Windows 11 computer.
2. Click on This PC in the left pane.
3. Under the Devices and drives section, double-click the device that contains the photos you want to import.
4. Navigate to the location of the images, such as This PC\Pixel 6 Pro\Internal shared storage\DCIM\Camera.
5. Select the images and videos you wish to import.
6. Right-click the selection and choose the Copy option.

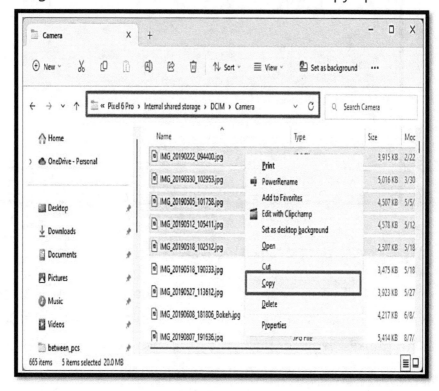

7. It's generally recommended to use the Copy option rather than Cut to prevent potential image loss in case of transfer failure.
8. Browse to the destination folder where you want to transfer the files.
9. Click the Paste option from the command bar.

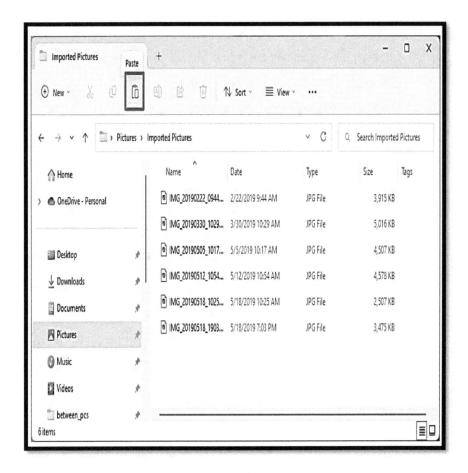

Import all pictures at once

Importing all your pictures at once is a convenient option, especially when dealing with a phone or camera. You can transfer all your photos using the File Explorer import feature by following these steps:

- Open File Explorer on your computer.
- In the left pane, click on This PC.
- Under the Devices and drives section, right-click the storage device that contains your photos (phone, camera, USB flash drive, or SD card). From the context menu, select the Import Pictures and Videos option.

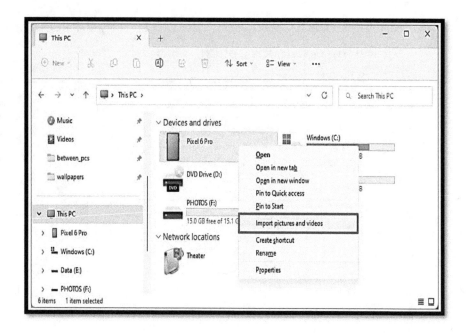

- A window for importing pictures and videos in File Explorer will appear.
- Click on More options.

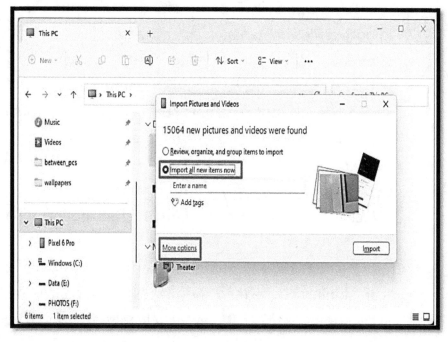

- Similarly, use the Browse button to specify a folder destination for the Import videos option.

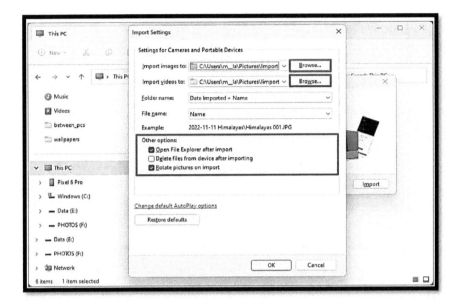

7. Under the Other Options section, you have several choices:
- Check the Open File Explorer after import option to access the imported files immediately after the transfer.
- (Optional) Check the Delete files from the device after importing option if you intend to free up space on the source storage device (note that this option is not recommended).
- (Optional) Check the Rotate pictures on the import option if needed.
- Click the OK button to confirm your settings.
- Select the Import all new items now an option to begin the import process.

NB: Choosing the Review, organizing, and group items to import option can significantly extend the process, especially when dealing with a large number of files. It may even lead to freezing if you have a substantial amount of data to transfer. Therefore, it is generally not recommended.

11. Click the Import button to initiate the transfer.

Upon completing these steps, all the images from your phone or camera will be transferred to your computer in one go.

Import photos from OneDrive

To import photos from your mobile device (such as an Android phone, iPhone, or iPad) to Windows 11, the easiest method is to upload the files to OneDrive and then access them from File Explorer. If you primarily use iCloud, you can also install the iCloud client for Windows 11 for a similar experience.

Follow these steps to import photos from your mobile device to Windows 11 using OneDrive:

1. Open the OneDrive app on your mobile device.
2. Tap the + (Plus) button located in the top-right corner and select the Upload option.
3. Choose the images you want to import and tap Select.

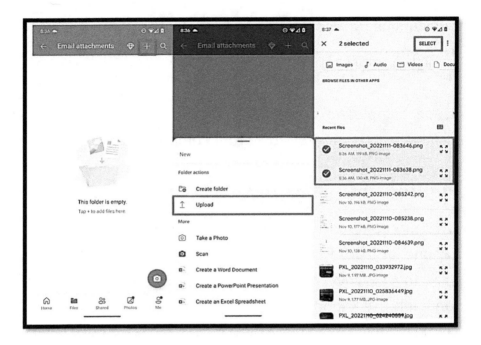

(For Android devices, the OneDrive import picture selection process may vary slightly.)

4. Open File Explorer.
5. Click on the OneDrive folder in the left pane.
6. Confirm that the selected pictures are available in your OneDrive folder.

Once you've completed these steps, the chosen images will be uploaded to the cloud and will become accessible in your OneDrive folder, provided you are signed in with the same Microsoft account on both your mobile device and your Windows 11 computer.

Enable Automatic Photo Transfer

OneDrive offers the convenience of automatically synchronizing your pictures and videos across multiple devices, eliminating the need for manual imports. To set up this automatic transfer feature, follow these steps:

1. Open the OneDrive app on your mobile device.
2. Tap the Me button located in the bottom-right corner.
3. Select Settings.
4. Choose Camera backup.
5. Tap the Backup device folders setting.
6. Check the folders containing pictures (e.g., Camera, Pictures, WhatsApp Images, etc.).

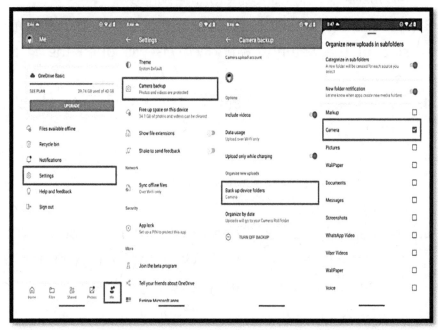

(Optional) Enable the New folder notification toggle switch if you want OneDrive to prompt you to transfer files when apps create new folders containing pictures.

Once you've completed these steps, any photos you capture with your mobile device will be automatically uploaded to OneDrive and synchronized seamlessly with your Windows 11 device.

Change an Image's Date

To change an image follow these instructions step by step

1. Begin by launching the Settings app.
2. On the left side of the Settings window, locate and click on the Time & language option. This will reveal settings related to time and language on the right side of the window.
3. Now, click on the Date & time option, which is found on the right side of the Settings window. This will open the Date & time settings.
4. You will see the current date and time displayed under the Current date and time setting.
5. If you wish to enable or disable the automatic time setting, toggle the switch for Set time automatically to your preferred position (On or Off).
6. To manually set the time you should choose to disable the automatic time setting and click on the Change button within the Set the date and time manually setting.
7. In the Change date and time window that appears, manually adjust the date and time to your desired values, and then click the Change button.
8. If you want to enable or disable automatic time zone setting, toggle the switch for Set time zone automatically to your preferred position (On or Off).
9. To enable or disable automatic adjustment for daylight saving time, in case you've disabled the automatic time zone setting, toggle the switch for Adjust for daylight saving time automatically to your desired position (On or Off).

10. If you need to set your time zone manually, select your desired time zone from the drop-down menu under the Time zone setting.

11. To manually synchronize the date and time with a Windows time server, click the Sync Now button within the Sync Now setting under the Additional Settings section.

12. If you wish to display additional calendars in the taskbar, make your selection from the drop-down menu in the Show additional calendars in the taskbar setting.

13. For those who require up to two additional clocks displaying different time zones, accessible when clicking or hovering over the taskbar clock, click on the Additional Clocks setting. This opens the Additional Clocks tab within the Date and Time dialog box.

14. To add a clock, check the Show this clock checkbox.

15. Select the desired time zone for the additional clock from the Select time zone drop-down menu.

16. Enter a display name for the clock in the Enter display name field.

17. If you need to add another clock, repeat steps 14 through 16.

18. Finally, click the OK button to add the additional clocks to the Windows taskbar.

19. To exit the Settings app, simply click the X button located in the upper-right corner when you've finished making your adjustments.

Sort Photos by Persons

To enable the facial grouping feature, which helps you organize your photos based on recognized faces, follow these step-by-step instructions:

1. **Access the Search Box:** To begin, make sure you are on your Windows desktop.

2. **Launch the Photos App:** Click or tap on the search box, and then type photos into it. As you start typing, you should see search results begin to appear. Among these results, you should find the Photos app. Click or tap on the Photos app to open it. This app is designed for viewing and managing your photos.

3. **Navigate to the People Tab:** Inside the Photos app, you'll see various tabs or options at the top. One of these tabs is labeled People. Click on the People tab to access the facial grouping settings.

4. **Access Settings**: In the upper-right corner of the Photos app window, you'll typically find a menu or options icon represented by three dots or lines. This icon is often used to access additional settings and features. Click or tap on this icon. It may be labeled as See More or More options.

5. **Enter Settings:** After clicking on the menu icon, a dropdown or side menu should appear. Look for an option labeled Settings within this menu and select it. This action will take you to the settings section of the Photos app.

6. **Toggle Facial Grouping**: Inside the settings, you'll find various sections and options. Look for the section related to Viewing and editing. In this section, there should be an option called People. This is the setting you want to toggle to enable facial grouping.

   • **Toggle the Setting**: To turn on the facial grouping feature, click or tap on the People setting. It may initially be set to Off. Click or tap it to switch it to the On position. When it's set to On, the app will start recognizing and grouping faces in your photos.

Adding Favorites

Adding Favorites in the Photos App on Windows:

1. **Launch the Photos App:** Begin by opening the Photos app on your computer. You can typically find it in your list of installed applications or search for it in the Windows Start menu.

2. **Select an Image:** Browse through your photo library within the Photos app and find an image that you want to mark as a favorite.

3. **Click on the Image:** Once you've located the image, click on it to open it in full view. This will display the selected image on your screen.

4. **Access the Top Menu Bar**: Look at the top of the Photos app window, and you'll see a menu bar with various options and icons.

5. **Add to Favorites:** In the top menu bar, there should be an option or icon that resembles a star or a heart, typically labeled as Add to Favorites or something similar. Click on this button. By doing so, you are designating the selected image as a favorite.

6. **Go to the Albums Tab**: Next, navigate to the Albums tab within the Photos app. This tab is usually located along the top or side of the app interface and is labeled as Albums.

7. **Find the Favorites Album:** Among the albums listed, you should see one labeled Favorites or My Favorites. Click on this album to access all the images you have marked as favorites.

8. **View Your Marked Images:** Once you're inside the Favorites album, you will find all the images you have designated as favorites. These are the pictures that you've selected for quick and easy access because they hold special significance or appeal to you.

Modify the look of the Photos App

Customizing the Appearance of the Photos App:

1. Open the Photos App: Start by launching the Photos app on your computer.

2. Access Settings: Once you have the Photos app open, direct your attention to the top-right corner of the app window. You should see an icon represented by three dots or lines. This icon typically indicates additional options or settings. Click on it to reveal a dropdown menu.

3. Select Settings: From the dropdown menu, locate and click on the Settings option. This action will take you to the settings menu of the Photos app.

4. Scroll to Appearance: In the Photos app settings, scroll down until you find the Appearance section. This section is where you can customize the overall look and feel of the app to suit your preferences.

5. Choose Your Preferred Look:

- **Light Mode**: If you prefer a brighter, more traditional appearance with white backgrounds and a lighter color scheme, select Light.
- **Dark Mode:** For a more visually comfortable and subdued look with darker backgrounds and text, choose Dark.
- **System Setting:** This option allows the Photos app to adapt its appearance based on your system-wide settings. If you have set your Windows system to light or dark mode, the Photos app will follow suit.

6. Apply Your Selection: After choosing your preferred appearance (Light, Dark, or System Setting), the Photos app will immediately update its look to reflect your choice.

Scanning Photos and Document

Scanning a Document or Photo on Windows 11:

1. Access the Search Function: Start by clicking on the search icon on your taskbar. This icon typically looks like a magnifying glass or a search bar, and it's located in the lower-left corner of your screen.

2. Search for Printers & Scanners: In the search bar, type Printers & scanners, and press Enter. This will open the system settings related to your printers and scanners.

3. Select Your Default Printer: In the Printers & scanners settings, you'll see a list of devices, including your default printer. Ensure that your printer is correctly connected to your computer. If it's not, Windows may not recognize it as an available scanning option. You can often find the default printer labeled as such.

4. Search for Fax and Scan: Once you've confirmed your printer is connected, return to the search bar by clicking on the search icon once more. This time, type Fax and scan and press Enter. This will initiate the Windows Fax and Scan utility.

5. Open the Windows Fax and Scan Utility: The Fax and Scan utility typically opens in a window that resembles a scanner interface.

6. Scan Your Document or Photo: You can now use this utility to scan your document or photo. Here's a basic outline of the process:

a. Choose New Scan: Look for an option like New Scan or Scan within the Fax and Scan window. Click on it to start the scanning process.

b. Select Scanner: If you have multiple scanning devices, you may need to choose the appropriate scanner from the list.

c. Configure Scan Settings: You can usually customize various scan settings, such as color mode, resolution, and file format. Adjust these settings to suit your needs.

d. Preview Scan: Many scanning utilities allow you to preview the scanned image before saving it. This helps make sure the scan looks as expected.

e. Scan Document or Photo: Click on the Scan or Start button to initiate the scan. Your scanner will feed the document or photo, and the software will process the image.

f. Save the Scan: Once the scan is complete, you'll have the option to save the scanned document or photo to your computer. Specify the destination folder and file name as needed.

g. Review and Edit: After saving, you can review and edit the scanned image if necessary. Many scanning utilities provide basic editing tools.

7. Close the Fax and Scan Utility: When you're finished scanning and saving your document or photo, you can close the Windows Fax and Scan utility.

Native Game

Built-in or pre-installed games that come with the operating system are referred to as native games. They don't necessitate any additional downloads or installations. Windows 11 includes several such native games that you can enjoy without any extra hassle. Here are some examples:

1. Solitaire Collection: This classic card game offers five different Solitaire variations: Klondike, Spider, FreeCell, Pyramid, and TriPeaks.

2. Minesweeper: In this logic puzzle game, your objective is to clear a board of hidden mines without triggering any of them.

3. Mahjong: A matching game where you must eliminate all tiles from the board by identifying pairs of identical tiles.

4. Sudoku: In this number puzzle game, your task is to fill a 9x9 grid with numbers from 1 to 9, ensuring that each row, column, and 3x3 subgrid contains each digit only once.

5. Jigsaw: A puzzle game where you need to assemble an image using a collection of pieces.

To access these native games follow these steps:

1. Open the Start Menu: Begin by opening the Start menu. You can typically do this by clicking on the Windows icon in the taskbar or pressing the Windows key on your keyboard.

2. Navigate to All Apps: In the Start menu, locate and click on the All Apps button located at the top-right corner. This will expand the menu to display all the apps and folders.

3. Find the Games Folder: Scroll through the list of apps and folders until you find the Games folder. Click on it to open and explore its contents.

4. Select Your Game: Inside the Games folder, you'll find a list of the native games available on your PC. Click on the one you wish to play.

5. Launch and Play: The selected game will launch in a new window. Here, you can adjust settings, choose a difficulty level, and start playing.

6. Pin to Start or Taskbar: If you have favorite games, you can pin them to the Start menu or the Taskbar for quick and convenient access. Right-click on the game icon and select Pin to Start or Pin to Taskbar.

MICROSOFT STORE

The Microsoft Store serves as a versatile platform where you can discover and download a diverse range of applications, games, movies, and TV shows for your PC. Windows 11 has introduced a revamped and enhanced Microsoft Store, aiming to deliver an improved user experience and a wider array of choices. Here are some of the standout features and advantages of the Microsoft Store:

1. Modern and Intuitive Interface: The Microsoft Store boasts a fresh, contemporary appearance that makes it more user-friendly. You can effortlessly explore the store through dedicated tabs for apps, games, and movies & TV shows. Additionally, the home screen showcases featured and recommended content. If you have a specific item in mind, the search bar simplifies the process of finding it.

2. Expanded App and Game Library: The Microsoft Store now offers an extensive catalog of apps and games, including some of the most popular titles from Android, Windows, and various other platforms. It also provides access to the Amazon App Store, allowing you to download Android apps directly to your PC. You'll find apps from diverse sources like Adobe Creative Cloud, Zoom, Disney+, TikTok, and more.

3. Enhanced Performance and Security: Performance and security have been prioritized in the new Microsoft Store. You can expect faster and more reliable downloads and installations of apps. Updates can be handled automatically or manually, offering greater convenience. Additionally, centralized app management tools empower you to fine-tune settings and permissions, all while ensuring that every app is safe and compatible with your PC.

4. Flexible Payment Options: The Microsoft Store offers versatility in payment methods. You can choose from various options such as credit cards, PayPal, gift cards, or even mobile carrier billing. Furthermore, you can benefit from discounts and special deals on apps, games, movies, and TV shows through services like Microsoft Rewards or Xbox Game Pass.

5. Seamless Accessibility: Accessing the Microsoft Store is a breeze. You can launch it by clicking on the Microsoft Store icon in the taskbar or by locating it within the Start menu under All Apps. This provides an easy and convenient way to personalize your PC with the apps and content that match your interests and needs.

How to Access the Microsoft Store

Using the Microsoft Store in Windows 11

Windows 11 brings a revamped Microsoft Store with improved navigation and support for third-party storefronts.

The Microsoft Store serves as the built-in platform for Windows users to access a variety of content, including apps, games, TV shows, and movies. With the transition to Windows 11, the Microsoft Store has undergone a significant redesign, making it easier for users to explore and locate the apps and media they require.

Notably, Microsoft is taking a significant step forward by allowing third-party storefronts to be accessible through the Microsoft Store. The first of these is the Epic Games Store, which provides a wide range of games and applications. Additionally, the Amazon Appstore, currently in beta, will enable Android apps to seamlessly function within Windows 11.

Here's a guide on how to navigate and utilize the Microsoft Store:

Accessing the Microsoft Store: On your computer, simply click on the Microsoft Store icon located in the taskbar to enter the storefront. The home screen presents various sections, including promoted apps, essential apps, free games, top free apps, trending apps, and collections. The Microsoft Store is further organized into tabs for apps, games, movies, and TV shows.

Exploring Apps:

- Click on the Apps icon in the left sidebar to browse both free and paid apps available for download. The page is divided into sections, showcasing special sales, best-selling apps, productivity tools, and collections.

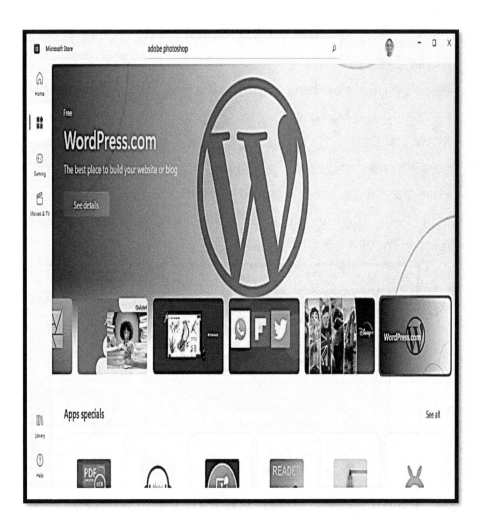

Discovering Games:

- Click the Gaming icon on the left and scroll through the screen to find free and paid games for download. This section highlights promoted games, best-sellers, top free games, top paid games, and various game collections.

Exploring Movies and TV Shows:

- To access films and TV shows, click on the Movies & TV icon on the left sidebar. Here, you can scroll through new movies, featured titles, new TV shows, top-selling TV shows, and collections of movies and TV series.

Efficient Search:

- Instead of navigating categories individually, you can efficiently search for your desired app, game, movie, or TV show. Simply enter your search term in the top search bar. You can further refine your search by selecting categories such as Apps, Games, Movies, or TV Shows.

Advanced Filters:

- Searches can be refined further using additional filters. Click the Filters button in the upper right corner to filter results by age group and type (free, paid, or on sale). Depending on the department selected, additional criteria such as category or subscription type can be used for filtering.

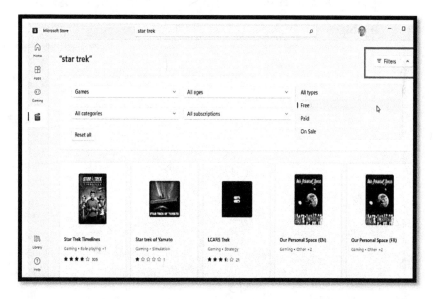

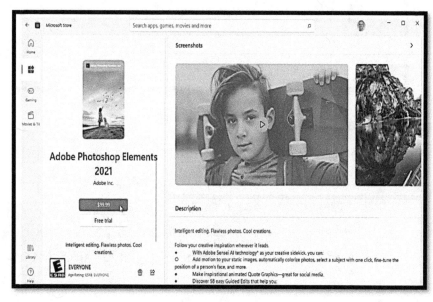

Managing Your Library:

- Once you've found an item you wish to download or purchase, select it. For free apps, click Get. For paid apps, click the button displaying the price.

- To monitor your downloads and purchases, click the Library icon at the bottom of the left sidebar. You can open a specific app by clicking Open, share it, pin it to the taskbar, or add it to the Start menu using the ellipsis icon.

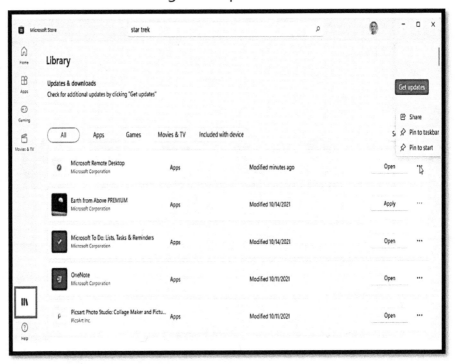

Updating Apps:

- Keep your apps up to date by clicking the Get Updates button to access the latest updates. If an app displays a cloud icon, it indicates you've downloaded the app on a different device. Click the cloud icon to download it to your current device. You can also sort your list of apps by date, name, installed, or not installed.

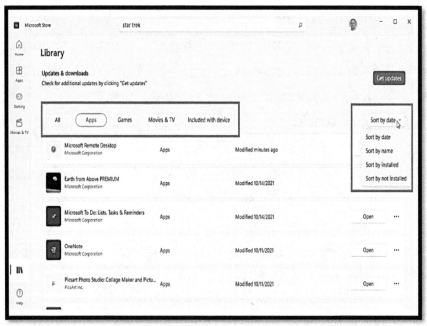

How to check the Categories

The Microsoft Store offers a diverse range of apps, games, movies, and TV shows, neatly organized into categories for easy discovery. Here's a step-by-step guide on how to browse these categories:

1. Accessing the Microsoft Store:
- Begin by launching the Microsoft Store app. You can do this by clicking on the Microsoft Store icon located in the taskbar or by searching for it in the Start menu.

2. Home Screen Sections:
- Upon opening the Microsoft Store, you'll land on the home screen. Here, you'll find various sections, including promoted apps, essential apps, free games, top free apps, trending apps, and collections.
- To explore more items within each section, simply scroll down on the home screen. If you wish to see an expanded list, click on See all within the respective section.

3. Category Icons:
- On the left sidebar of the Microsoft Store window, you'll find icons representing different categories, including apps, games, and movies & TV shows.
- Click on any of these icons to switch to the corresponding category and begin exploring the content within it.

4. Subcategories and Filters:
- Within each category page, you'll encounter subcategories that allow you to refine your search.
- For example, in the Apps category, you can filter by best-selling apps, productivity tools, utilities, and more.

- In the Games category, you can narrow down your options by selecting from subcategories like top free games, top paid games, casual games, and others.
- Similarly, in the Movies and TV Shows category, you can filter by criteria such as new releases, featured movies, specific genres, and more.

5. Search Functionality:

- To find a particular app, game, movie, or TV show quickly, utilize the search bar located at the top of the Microsoft Store window.
- Type the name or relevant keywords into the search bar and hit Enter. You can further refine your search by selecting a specific category from the drop-down menu adjacent to the search bar.

Choosing an App from the App Store

Selecting an application from the Microsoft App Store on Windows 11 might vary a bit compared to prior Windows versions. To assist you in locating and installing your desired app, here are step-by-step instructions:

1. Access the App Store: To begin, open the App Store. You can achieve this by clicking the Start button and then selecting the App Store icon located on the right-hand side of the menu. Alternatively, you can use the shortcut by pressing the Windows logo key + S and entering the App Store in the search box.

2. Search or Explore: Next, you'll need to either search for your desired app or explore available options. You can utilize the tabs situated at the top of the App Store window to browse through various app categories such as Games, Entertainment, Productivity, and more.

Additionally, you can employ the search box at the top right corner to enter the app's name or relevant keywords.

3. Choose Your App: Once you've located the app you want, take action accordingly. If the app is free, simply click on the Get button. For paid apps, select the button displaying the price. You may be required to sign in using your Microsoft account or create one if you don't already have it.

4. Launch Your App: Finally, launch the app you've installed. You can do this by clicking the Launch button on the app's page within the App Store. Alternatively, you can locate the app in your Start menu or on your taskbar. To ensure easy access, consider pinning the app to your Start menu or taskbar.

Checking for available Update

To verify and install updates from the Microsoft Store, follow these steps:

1. Open the Microsoft Store: Launch the Microsoft Store application, typically accessible on the taskbar or within the Start menu.

2. Access Your Library: Click on the Library icon located on the left-hand side of the Microsoft Store interface.

3. Check for Updates: Locate the Get Updates button situated at the top right corner, just above your list of installed apps.

4. Initiate Update Check: Clicking the Get Updates button will prompt the Microsoft Store to immediately scan for available updates for your installed applications and games.

5. Automatic Updates: If there are updates available for your apps or games, they will commence downloading and installing automatically.

6. Manage Updates: If necessary, you can click on the More actions button (represented by three dots) next to specific apps and games to perform actions like canceling or downloading updates immediately.

7. Complete the Process: Once all updates have been installed or managed to your satisfaction, you can choose to close the Microsoft Store application if desired.

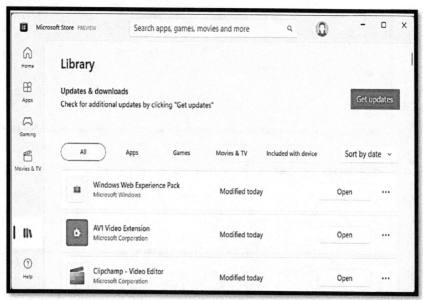

Enabling Automatic App Updates

To activate and ensure automatic updates for your apps follow these instructions:

1. Launch Microsoft Store: Open the Microsoft Store application.

2. Access App Settings: Click the profile menu button, then choose the App settings option.

3. Enable App Updates: In the app settings, toggle the switch labeled App updates to the ON position. This action activates automatic updates for apps on your system.

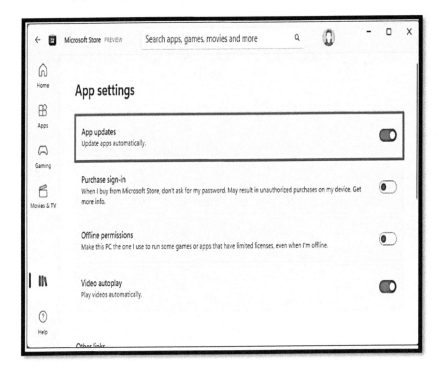

Once you've completed these steps, your apps will receive automatic updates. Keep in mind that there might be a delay before updates are applied after a new release becomes available.

Clicking the context menu

The context menu within the Microsoft Store on Windows 11 is a menu that materializes when you right-click on an app or game within the store interface. This menu provides a range of actions you can take, such as installing, uninstalling, launching, rating, sharing, or pinning the app or game to your Start menu or taskbar.

To access the context menu within the Microsoft Store follow these steps:

1. Launch the Microsoft Store App: Initiate the Microsoft Store app by clicking on the Start button and selecting the App Store icon located on the right side of the menu. Alternatively, you can expedite this process by pressing the Windows logo key + S and typing App Store into the search box.

2. Browse or Search for Your App or Game: Locate the app or game you desire by exploring the various categories of apps and games using the tabs at the top of the App Store window (e.g., Games, Entertainment, Productivity, etc.) or by using the search box at the top right corner to input the app or game's name or keywords.

3. Invoke the Context Menu: Right-click on the app or game you're interested in. A context menu will appear, offering a selection of options. The specific options you see will depend on whether you have already installed the app or game. For instance, if it's not yet installed, options like Get, Install on my devices, Share, Pin to Start, and Pin to Taskbar may be available. If it's already installed, options such as

Launch, Uninstall, Rate and Review, Share, Pin to Start, and Pin to Taskbar could be presented.

4. Execute Your Chosen Action: Click on the desired option from the context menu to perform the action you intend to take. The chosen action will then be carried out accordingly.

Checking the App Settings

To access and configure app settings within the Microsoft Store, follow these simple steps:

1. Open the Microsoft Store App: Initiate the Microsoft Store app.

2. Access Your Profile: Locate your profile icon positioned at the top right corner of the app window. This icon may display your Microsoft account picture or a generic symbol.

3. Navigate to App Settings: Click on the App settings option from the menu that appears. This action will open a new window offering a variety of options for customizing your app experience.

Within the App settings window, you can make adjustments to the following settings:

- **Update apps automatically:** Toggle this setting on or off to decide whether you prefer your apps to be automatically updated or if you want to manage updates manually.
- **Require password for purchases:** Toggle this setting on or off to determine whether you'd like to enter your Microsoft account password each time you purchase in the store.
- **Offline permissions:** Toggle this setting on or off to specify whether you want your device to run apps and games when offline. Additionally, you can manage your offline devices from this section.

- **Video autoplay**: Toggle this setting on or off to control whether videos automatically play when you browse the store.
- **Clear cache:** Click the Clear cache button to purge the store app's cache, freeing up storage space on your device.
- **Reset:** Click the Reset button to restore the store app to its default settings. This action may resolve certain issues you may encounter with the app.

How to Add a Payment Method

To add a payment method within the Microsoft Store, follow these steps:

1. Open the Microsoft Store App: Begin by launching the Microsoft Store app.

2. Access Your Profile: Locate your profile icon, which is typically situated at the top right corner of the app window. This icon may display your Microsoft account picture or a generic symbol.

3. Navigate to App Settings: Click on the App settings option from the menu that appears. This action will open a new window presenting various options to tailor your app experience.

4. Select Payment Methods: Inside the App settings window, click on the Payment Methods tab found on the left-hand side. This section will display your current payment methods and allow you to add new ones.

5. Add a Payment Method: Click on the Add a Payment Method button located at the top right of the window. This will initiate a new window where you can choose the type of payment method you wish to add, such as a credit card, debit card, PayPal, or mobile phone.

6. Provide Required Information: Fill in the necessary information for your selected payment method and then click Save. You may be prompted to sign in with your Microsoft account or create one if you haven't already.

7. Confirmation: Your newly added payment method will now appear in your list of payment methods. You can conveniently use it for your upcoming purchases within the Microsoft Store.

Using payment Codes

Utilizing payment codes in the Microsoft Store provides an alternative method for acquiring apps, games, movies, and TV shows, bypassing the need for a credit card or other traditional payment methods.

How to Redeem Codes or Gift Cards In Microsoft Windows 11

Microsoft offers gift cards and codes that can be redeemed and used on the Microsoft online store, Xbox, and other Microsoft services to acquire a wide range of Microsoft products and devices. These gift cards function similarly to traditional brand-specific gift cards, allowing you to make purchases using them.

These gift codes and cards can be obtained in the form of vouchers, often issued as a means of making online purchases or payments. Think of these gift codes as digital gift coupons that enable you to shop or spend funds through specific websites or applications within the Microsoft ecosystem.

Redeeming Microsoft Gift Cards through the Microsoft Store is a straightforward process. Ensure you have a stable internet connection, and your Windows-operated device is connected to the internet. Follow these steps to redeem your gift card:

1. Access the Microsoft Store:

- To begin, access the Start menu or use the search bar located on your Windows operating system's home screen.

2. Search for Microsoft Store:

- In the search bar, type Microsoft Store or simply Store.

3. Open the Microsoft Store:

- Once you locate the Microsoft Store, double-click on the application to open it.

4. Access Your Profile:

- On the top right corner of the Microsoft Store's home page, you'll find the Profile option. Click on it.

5. Redeem Codes or Gift Cards:

- In your Microsoft account profile menu, you'll find an option that says Redeem your code or gift cards. Click on this option.

6. Enter the 25-Digit Code:

- A dialogue box will appear, prompting you to enter your 25-digit code.

7. Code Entry Options:

- Enter the complete 25-digit code manually, ensuring accuracy.
- Alternatively, you can scan the QR code on your gift card to redeem it.

8. Confirmation:
- After entering the code or scanning it, click on the Next option. This will open a new dialogue box asking for confirmation to redeem the gift card.

9. Confirm Redemption:
- Click on the Confirm button to proceed with the redemption process.

10. Redemption Complete:
- Your gift card will be successfully redeemed, and the credited amount will be added to your Microsoft account balance. You can then use this balance to make purchases.

Using Online Method To Redeem Microsoft Gift Cards

Using the Online Method to Redeem Microsoft Gift Cards is a viable alternative, especially when the Microsoft Store is not functioning correctly. This method involves accessing the Microsoft website and logging into your account to complete the redemption process. Here's a step-by-step guide:

1. Prepare Your Information:
- Ensure you have your Microsoft account ID and password ready.
- Make sure your device is connected to a stable internet connection.

2. Launch Your Web Browser:

- Open your preferred web browser on your device.

3. Access Microsoft's Redemption Page:
- In your browser, either perform a search for the Microsoft redemption page for gift cards or click on the following link (insert link).

4. Log into Your Microsoft Account:
- On the Microsoft gift card redemption website, log in to your account using your Microsoft ID and password.

5. Enter the 25-Digit Code:
- Similar to the Microsoft Store method, you will encounter a box where you need to input the 25-digit code from your gift card.

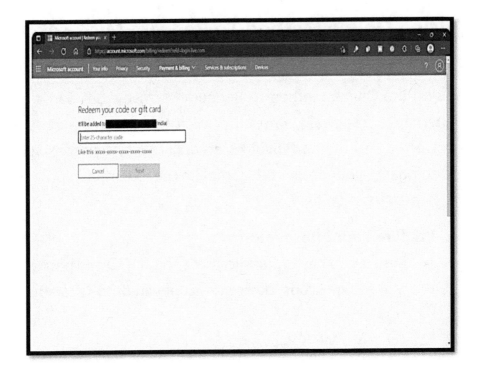

7. Code Entry:

- Enter the complete 25-digit code accurately.

8. Confirmation Pop-up:

- After entering the code, click on the Next button or its equivalent to proceed.

9. Confirm Redemption:

- A pop-up window will appear, asking you to confirm the redemption. Click on the Confirm button to finalize the process.

Purchasing TV series and films

To buy TV series and films from the Microsoft Store, simply follow these steps:

1. Access the Microsoft Store:

- Open the Microsoft Store app by clicking on the Start button and selecting the App Store icon from the menu.

2. Navigate to Movies & TV:

- On the left sidebar, locate and click on the Movies & TV icon. Here, you can explore various categories, including new movies, featured movies, new TV shows, top-selling TV shows, and collections of movies and TV series.

3. Choose Your Content:

- Select the specific movie or TV show you wish to purchase. You can also utilize the search box at the top right corner to quickly find your desired content.

4. Make the Purchase:

- Click on the button displaying the price to buy the movie or TV show. If necessary, sign in with your Microsoft account or create one if you don't already have an account.

5. Access Your Content:

- After completing the purchase, you can watch your selected movie or TV show using the Movies & TV app on your Windows device or Xbox console.

6. Offline Viewing:

- If you prefer, you can also download the content to your device for offline viewing, allowing you to enjoy your movie or TV show even without an internet connection.

Managing the store Account

For comprehensive management of your Microsoft Store apps, devices, and accounts, follow these steps:

1. Click on your profile icon.

2. Select Manage account and devices.

3. This action will open the website for your Microsoft account, where you can perform various tasks such as canceling or renewing subscriptions and viewing or unlinking any connected devices.

How to Listen to Music

Music Streaming

Music streaming is the practice of enjoying music online without the need to download it to your device. Windows 11 offers a variety of apps available in the Microsoft Store that facilitate music streaming from diverse sources like Spotify, iTunes, Musixmatch, and more. These applications offer an array of features, including online music streaming, music library synchronization across devices, lyrics display, and playlist creation.

Benefits of music streaming include:

1. **Access to a Vast Music Library**: You can explore an extensive and diverse collection of music spanning various genres, artists, and countries.

2. **Music Discovery:** Discover new music based on your preferences, current mood, or activities.

3. **Storage Conservation:** Save storage space on your device as you don't need to download music files.

4. **Offline Listening**: Download songs or playlists for offline listening, allowing you to enjoy your favorite tunes without an internet connection.

5. **Sharing Music**: Easily share your music with friends and family through social media or messaging apps.

Drawbacks of music streaming include:

1. **Internet Dependency**: To stream music without interruptions or buffering, a stable and high-speed internet connection is often necessary.

2. **Subscription Costs or Ads**: Some music streaming services require a subscription fee or serve ads to access specific features or content.

3. **Licensing and Regional Restrictions**: Certain songs or albums may not be available for streaming due to licensing agreements or regional limitations.

4. **Limited Control Over Quality**: You may not have full control over the audio quality or format of the music you stream, depending on the service and your subscription tier.

Groove Music and Windows Media Player

Groove Music and Windows Media Player are distinct applications designed for playing music files on Windows devices. Here are the key differences between them:

1. Platform Compatibility:

- Groove Music is a Universal Windows app, compatible with a range of Windows 10 devices, including PCs, tablets, phones, and Xbox One.
- Windows Media Player, on the other hand, is a desktop application primarily designed for use on PCs.

2. User Interface Design:

- Groove Music boasts a modern and sleek design in line with the Windows 10 style.
- Windows Media Player features a more traditional and older interface reminiscent of previous Windows versions.

3. Music Sources:

- Groove Music can stream music from online services like Spotify, iTunes, and Musixmatch in addition to playing local files.
- Windows Media Player is primarily geared toward local music files and online radio stations.

4. Music Library Sync:

- Groove Music allows for music library and playlist synchronization across devices, including those linked to your Microsoft account.
- Windows Media Player supports music synchronization with devices via USB or Wi-Fi but lacks cloud-based syncing features.

5. Media Information Display:

- Groove Music offers detailed song information, including lyrics, album art, and artist imagery.
- Windows Media Player provides basic song details like title, artist, and genre.

6. Audio Format Compatibility:

- Groove Music can play a variety of audio formats, including MP3, FLAC, OGG, WAV, and more.
- Windows Media Player also supports multiple audio formats, though additional codecs may be required for some formats.

7. Video Playback:

- Groove Music is primarily focused on music playback but can also handle video files.
- Windows Media Player is a comprehensive multimedia player capable of playing both audio and video files, offering a wider range of features and options for video playback.

VLC Media

To enjoy music with VLC Media through the Microsoft Store, it's essential to understand that VLC Media is a free and open-source media player capable of playing nearly any audio or video file format without the need for additional codecs. It also enables you to stream online radio stations, podcasts, and various audio sources.

To download and install VLC Media from the Microsoft Store, follow these steps:

1. Access the Microsoft Store App:

- Launch the Microsoft Store app by clicking the Start button and selecting the App Store icon located on the right side of the menu. Alternatively, use the Windows logo key + S shortcut and search for App Store.

2. Find VLC Media:

- Search for VLC Media by using the tabs at the top of the App Store window to explore different app categories, such as Games, Entertainment, Productivity, etc. Alternatively, you can use the search box in the top right corner to type VLC Media or relevant keywords.

3. Select and Install VLC Media:

- Choose VLC Media from the search results. For free apps, click the Get button. For paid apps, click the button displaying the price. You may be prompted to sign in with your Microsoft account or create one if needed.

4. Launch VLC Media:
- Once the installation is complete, you can launch VLC Media from your Start menu or taskbar. You can then play your music files stored on your device or network share.

To stream music from online sources using VLC Media, follow these steps:

1. Open VLC Media.

2. Navigate to Media:
- Click on the Media menu and select the Stream option.

3. Add Media Source:
- In the File tab, click the Add button to choose the file you want to stream with VLC Media. Alternatively, under the Network tab, enter the URL of the online radio station, podcast, or audio source you wish to stream.

4. Configure Streaming:

- Click Stream and follow the wizard to configure your streaming options. You can specify the destination of your stream (e.g., a file, display, or network address) and adjust transcoding settings, including codec, bitrate, resolution, and frame rate.

5. Start Streaming:

- Click Stream again to commence streaming your chosen music source in VLC Media.

CONCLUSION

Windows 11 offers a versatile and user-friendly set of tools and features for taking, viewing, editing, and organizing photos and videos. These functionalities are integrated seamlessly into the operating system, providing a holistic multimedia experience for users. In summary, it enhances the multimedia experience by providing integrated tools and features for capturing, viewing, editing, and organizing photos and videos. Whether you're a casual user looking to browse and share memories or a more advanced user interested in editing and creative projects, Windows 11's multimedia capabilities cater to a wide range of needs and preferences, making it a versatile platform for managing your digital media.

CHAPTER TWELVE

TIPS, TRICKS AND TROUBLESHOOTING

Printer Troubleshooting

When encountering printer problems whether you have an HP, Canon, Epson, or any other brand of printer, the issues can stem from a variety of sources. Potential culprits include connectivity disruptions caused by software glitches or physical connection problems. Driver issues or hiccups in the print spooler can also be responsible. Furthermore, it's possible that you inadvertently directed your print job to the wrong printer, among other potential complications.

Irrespective of the specific problem, there are numerous troubleshooting steps you can take to address printing issues on Windows 11. These range from basic actions like rebooting your devices and inspecting physical connections to more advanced solutions such as utilizing built-in troubleshooters, resetting the printer spooler, or even reinstalling the printer driver. By systematically exploring these options, you can increase your chances of resolving the printing problem and restoring seamless functionality to your printer.

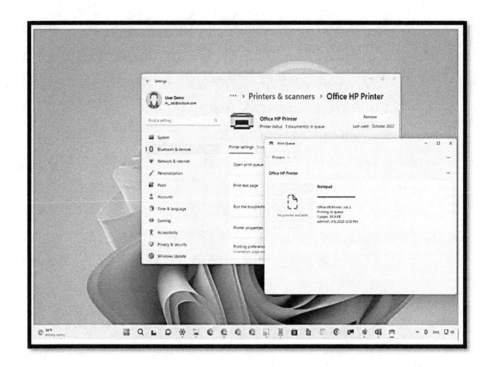

To troubleshoot printer problems using the troubleshooter option, follow these step-by-step instructions:

Here are steps to address common printer issues on Windows 11, including methods to troubleshoot and resolve them:

1. Restart Printer Method:
- Sometimes, a simple restart can resolve common printer problems. Turn off the printer, unplug its power source, wait for a moment, then plug it back in and turn it on.
- After restarting the printer, try to print again. If the issue persists, consider restarting your computer as well before attempting to print.

2. Check Connection Method:
- For USB printers, ensure the data cable is securely connected to both the printer and the computer. Try disconnecting and reconnecting the cable or using a different USB port.

- If you have a wireless printer, ensure that the wireless functionality is enabled on the printer and check for a solid wireless connection. Consult your printer's manual or manufacturer for specific instructions.
- If you encounter connectivity problems with other wireless devices, you may need to restart your router or access point to resolve the issue.

3. Configure Default Printer Method:

- If you have multiple printers installed on your computer, you might be inadvertently sending print jobs to the wrong default printer.
- To change the default printer settings on Windows 11:
- Open Settings.
- Click on Bluetooth & devices.
- Navigate to the Printers & scanners tab.

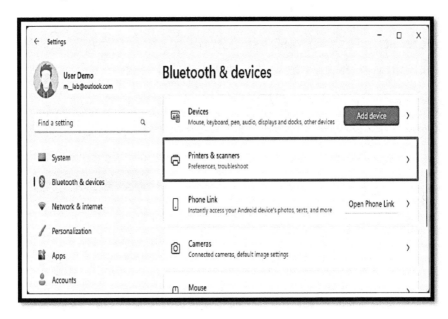

- Under Printer preferences, turn off Let Windows manage my default printer.

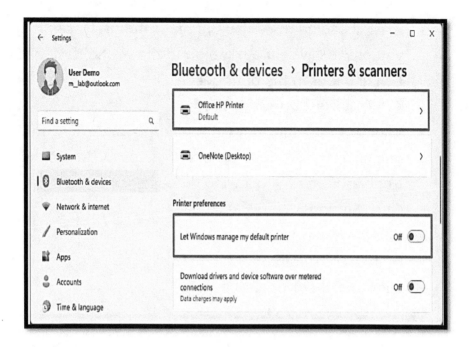

- Select the desired printer from the list.
- Click Set as default.

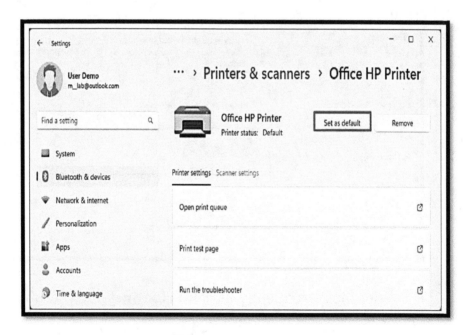

- After changing the default printer settings, try printing again. If you previously sent a print job to the wrong device, cancel any pending jobs in the print queue.

4. Printer Troubleshooter Method:

- Windows 11 includes troubleshooters to automatically diagnose and fix common issues. Run the Printer troubleshooter by following these steps:
- Open Settings.
- Click on System.
- Go to the Troubleshoot tab.
- Click on Other troubleshooters.

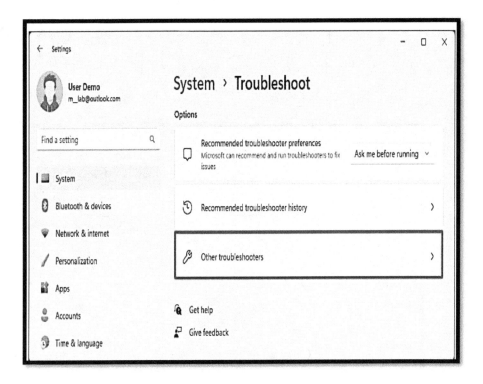

- Under Most Frequently, click Run for the Printer troubleshooter.

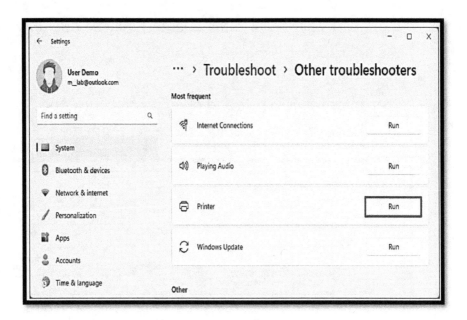

- Select the printer (if applicable).

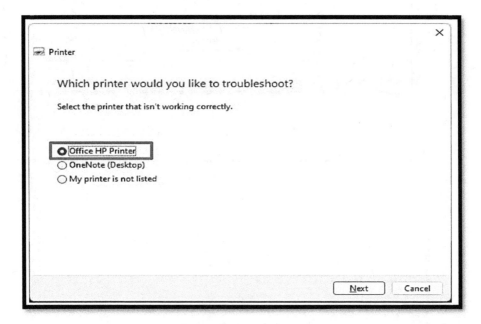

- Follow on-screen instructions to complete the troubleshooting process.

5. Reset Printer Spooler Method:

- If print jobs get stuck in the queue, it may be due to issues with the print spooler service.
- Open Start.
- Search for services.msc and open it.
- Right-click on Print Spooler and select Properties.

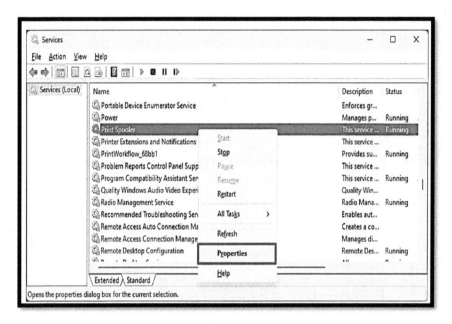

- In the General tab, click Stop to stop the service.

- Use the Windows key + R keyboard shortcut to open the Run command, then type C:\Windows\System32\spool\printers and press Enter.
- Select all items in the printer's folder (Ctrl + A) and delete them.

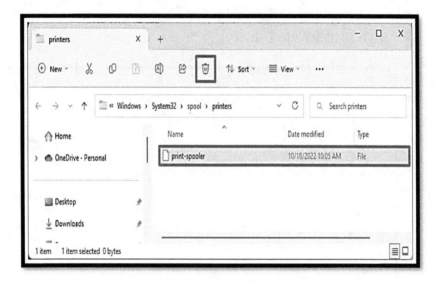

- Return to the Printer Spooler Properties window, click Start to restart the service, and then click OK.

6. Reinstall Printer Method:

- If the printer issue is related to driver problems, you can try uninstalling and reinstalling the printer driver.
- Open Settings.
- Click on Bluetooth & devices.
- Navigate to the Printers & scanners page.

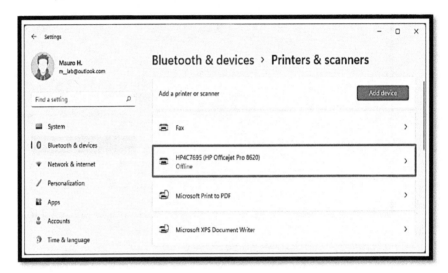

- Select the printer you want to remove and click Remove.

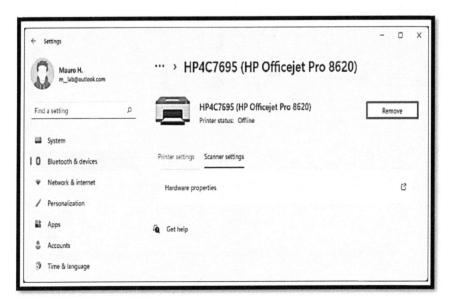

- Confirm by clicking Yes.

After completing these steps, you can reinstall the printer driver if needed.

Wireless and Internet Troubleshooting

Windows 11 offers a plethora of offline features, yet many critical functions rely heavily on a stable internet connection. When connectivity issues arise, they can be incredibly frustrating. Here's what you can do to troubleshoot and resolve internet-related problems:

1. Check Other Devices:

Begin by checking your other internet-connected devices. If none of them are working, it could indicate an issue with your router or a local outage in your area.

2. Restart Your Device and Ensure Wi-Fi is On:

- A simple and effective solution is to restart your computer. Click the Start menu, then the power button in the bottom right, and select Restart.
- Ensure that Wi-Fi is enabled. Head to Settings > Network & Internet and confirm that the Wi-Fi toggle is switched on.

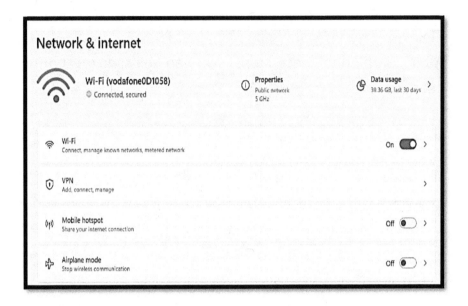

3. Disable and Re-enable Wi-Fi Adapter:

- Updates can sometimes affect Wi-Fi settings. Navigate to Settings > Network & Internet > Advanced network settings, then click Disable followed by Enable.

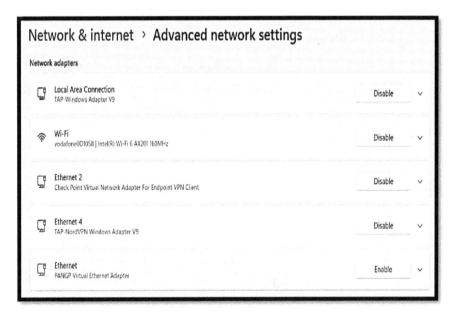

4. Reset Known Networks:

- Try forgetting your network and re-entering the connection details manually. Go to Settings > Network & Internet > Wi-Fi > Manage known networks and click Forget next to your usual network.

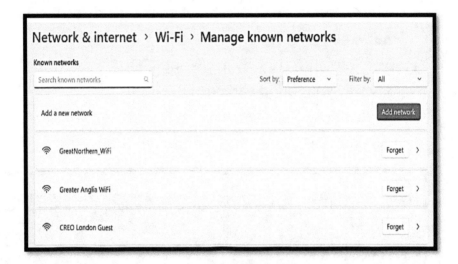

- Return to the main Wi-Fi page, select your network from the Show available networks drop-down, enter your password, and reconnect.

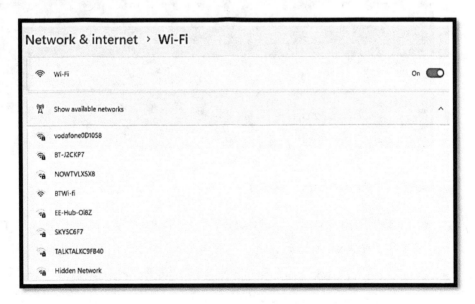

5. Perform a Network Connection Test:

- To determine if the issue is related to your computer's connection to the router, open Command Prompt by searching for it in the Start menu.
- Type 'ipconfig' and hit Enter, then find the 'Default Gateway' for the wireless network.
- Type 'ping ROUTER-IP,' replacing 'ROUTER-IP' with the Default Gateway you found earlier.
- Confirm that 4 packets have been sent and received. If not, the issue may be related to your internet provider.

```
Command Prompt          ×    +  ∨

   Connection-specific DNS Suffix  . :

Wireless LAN adapter Wi-Fi:

   Connection-specific DNS Suffix  . : broadband
   Link-local IPv6 Address . . . . . : fe80::3dfd:6395:39aa:57fa%13
   IPv4 Address. . . . . . . . . . . : 192.168.1.24
   Subnet Mask . . . . . . . . . . . : 255.255.255.0
   Default Gateway . . . . . . . . . : 192.168.1.1

Ethernet adapter vEthernet (Default Switch):

   Connection-specific DNS Suffix  . :
   Link-local IPv6 Address . . . . . : fe80::556f:80db:561b:fcfc%44
   IPv4 Address. . . . . . . . . . . : 172.18.144.1
   Subnet Mask . . . . . . . . . . . : 255.255.240.0
   Default Gateway . . . . . . . . . :

C:\Users\anyron_copeman>ping 192.168.1.1

Pinging 192.168.1.1 with 32 bytes of data:
Reply from 192.168.1.1: bytes=32 time=1ms TTL=64
Reply from 192.168.1.1: bytes=32 time=1ms TTL=64
Reply from 192.168.1.1: bytes=32 time=1ms TTL=64
Reply from 192.168.1.1: bytes=32 time<1ms TTL=64

Ping statistics for 192.168.1.1:
    Packets: Sent = 4, Received = 4, Lost = 0 (0% loss),
Approximate round trip times in milli-seconds:
    Minimum = 0ms, Maximum = 1ms, Average = 0ms
```

6. Reset Networking Stack:

- Resetting the Windows 11 network stack can resolve configuration errors. Open Command Prompt as an administrator and enter the following commands one by one, hitting Enter after each:

294

- netsh winsock reset
- netsh int ip reset
- ipconfig /release
- ipconfig /renew
- ipconfig /flushdns

```
Administrator: Command Prompt

Wireless LAN adapter Wi-Fi:

    Connection-specific DNS Suffix  . : broadband
    Link-local IPv6 Address . . . . . : fe80::3dfd:6395:39aa:57fa%13
    IPv4 Address. . . . . . . . . . . : 192.168.1.24
    Subnet Mask . . . . . . . . . . . : 255.255.255.0
    Default Gateway . . . . . . . . . : 192.168.1.1

Ethernet adapter vEthernet (Default Switch):

    Connection-specific DNS Suffix  . :
    Link-local IPv6 Address . . . . . : fe80::556f:80db:561b:fcfc%44
    IPv4 Address. . . . . . . . . . . : 172.18.144.1
    Subnet Mask . . . . . . . . . . . : 255.255.240.0
    Default Gateway . . . . . . . . . :

C:\Windows\System32>ipconfig /flushdns

Windows IP Configuration

Successfully flushed the DNS Resolver Cache.

C:\Windows\System32>
```

- Restart your device to apply the changes.

7. Use Windows 11 Troubleshooter:

- Windows 11 features a built-in troubleshooter for common issues. Try the Internet Connections troubleshooter by going to Settings > System > Troubleshoot > Other troubleshooters. Click Run next to Internet Connections and follow the instructions.

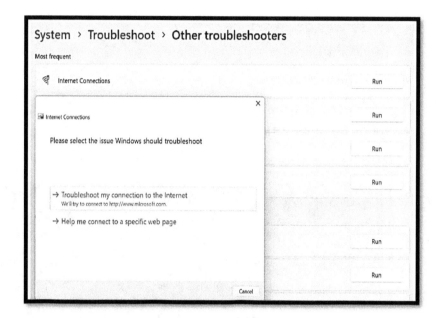

8. Reset the Entire Network:

- All network settings to factory defaults can often resolve complex issues. Head to Settings > Network & Internet > Advanced network settings > Network reset and click Reset now. Your device will restart once this is complete.

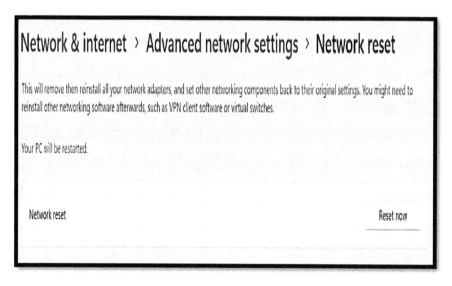

9. Update Drivers:

- Outdated drivers can affect your internet connection. If you can connect to another Wi-Fi network (e.g., your phone's hotspot), try installing any pending driver updates.

- Go to Settings > Windows Update > Advanced options > Optional updates, then select any driver updates and choose Download & install.

- If you're still experiencing issues, manually update drivers via Device Manager. Open the app, click the Network adapters drop-down, right-click each one, and select Update driver. Ensure you know the location of available drivers on your computer.

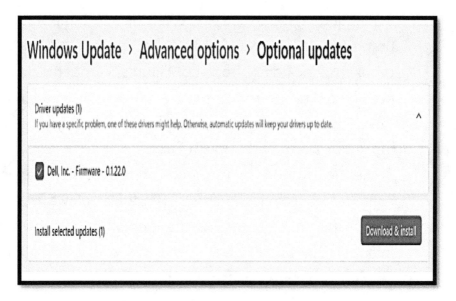

Error Messages, Crashes and Freezing Issues

The freezing issues can be caused by a variety of factors, including outdated GPU drivers, insufficient RAM, corrupt system files, and conflicting programs or apps. Let's delve into the details of these potential causes:

1. Outdated or Incompatible GPU Drivers:

- If your computer is running on outdated, corrupted, or incompatible GPU drivers, it can lead to freezing problems. These drivers are essential for rendering graphics, and any issues with them can result in system instability.

- Additionally, compatibility problems between GPU drivers and Windows updates, such as the 21H2 update (KB5021255), can trigger freezing issues.

2. Insufficient RAM:

- Inadequate system memory, often due to temporary files and unwanted data consuming valuable space, can lead to various problems, including boot-up failures, frequent crashes, and even blue screen errors. Insufficient RAM may result in Windows freezing.

3. Corrupted or Damaged System Files:

- Broken, corrupted, or missing system files can be significant contributors to freezing issues. These files play a crucial role in the proper functioning of the operating system, and their integrity is essential.

4. Conflicting Programs/Apps:

- Certain programs or apps, especially those related to gaming, can conflict with the operating system, leading to system freezes. For example, problematic applications like Sonic Studio 3 can disrupt system stability when they don't function correctly.

Now, let's explore potential solutions to address Windows 11 freezing issues.

Quick Fixes

1. Close Unresponsive Apps With Task Manager:

- When specific applications or programs become unresponsive, you can use Task Manager to close them. This is effective when the program is frozen, but the rest of the system is responsive.

- To access Task Manager, simultaneously press the CTRL+ALT+DEL keys and select Task Manager from the available options. Choose the unresponsive program, application, or software, and then click on End Task to terminate it.

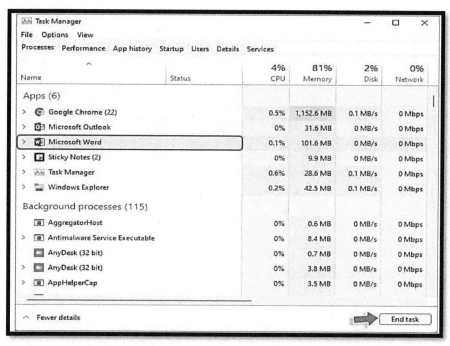

- You may also encounter the Restart option. If it appears, select it after choosing the application or program, and then proceed to restart it.

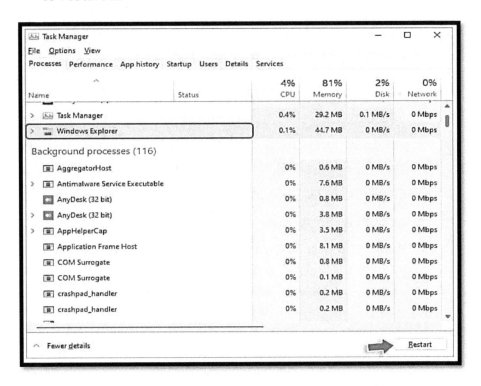

2. Force Shut Down and Reboot System:

- In cases where your system becomes unresponsive, a force shutdown can be attempted. However, this should be done sparingly, as frequent forced shutdowns can harm your OS and system drive.

Advanced Fixes

3. Update GPU Drivers:

- Updating your GPU (Graphics Processing Unit) drivers to the latest compatible versions is crucial. Outdated or incompatible

GPU drivers can cause freezing, especially when using graphics-intensive applications or games.

- Access Device Manager through the Start menu and expand the Display adapters category. Afterward, right-click on the graphics driver and select the Update driver option.

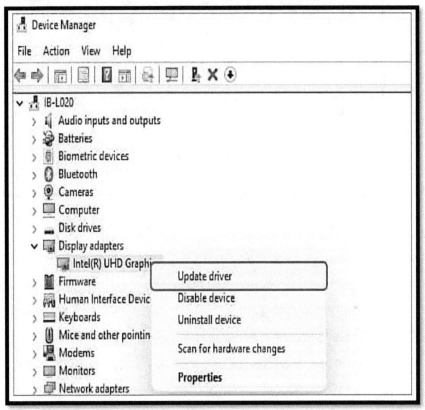

- Now, click on Search automatically for drivers. Windows will search for and download any available updated driver software for the device if it's accessible.

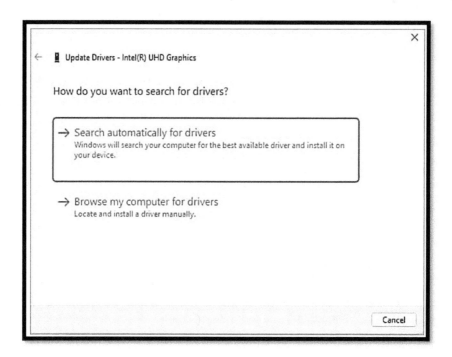

4. Change Screen Resolution:

- Altering your screen resolution can help resolve freezing issues. Sometimes, the current resolution settings can cause problems, particularly if they don't align with your graphics hardware.

- Access System Settings by pressing Windows + I, and then navigate to System followed by Display. You can modify the display resolution using the Scale and Layout option found in the right panel.

5. Delete Temporary Files:

- Regularly deleting temporary files can free up valuable system memory. These files can accumulate over time and consume unnecessary space, potentially contributing to freezing issues.

- Launch File Explorer by pressing Windows + E, and then navigate to This PC. Next, right-click on the C: drive and choose Properties.

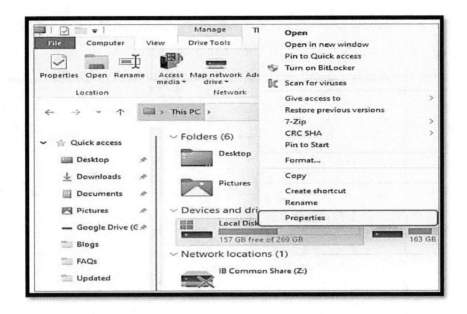

- Now, select Disk Cleanup from the options available under the General tab.

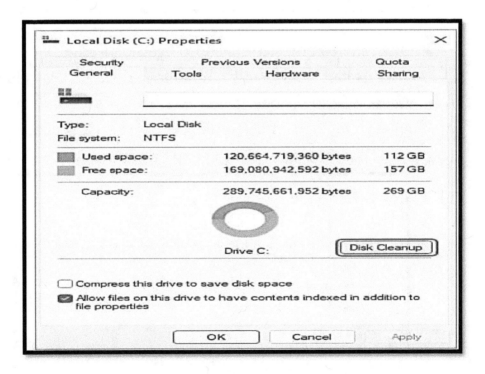

- Choose the files you wish to remove from the Temporary files category, and then click on the OK button.

- After completing the cleanup process, close the window, and then restart your system to determine if the Windows 11 freezing issue has been resolved.

An alternative method to delete temporary files is by accessing the Run dialog box (Windows + R), entering %temp%, and pressing Enter.

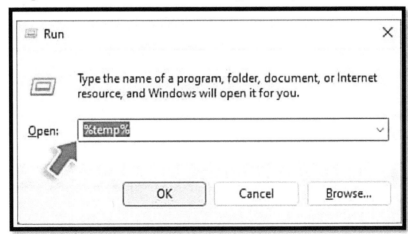

This action will open the Temp folder, allowing you to select all the temporary files, and then you can press Shift + Del to permanently delete them from your system.

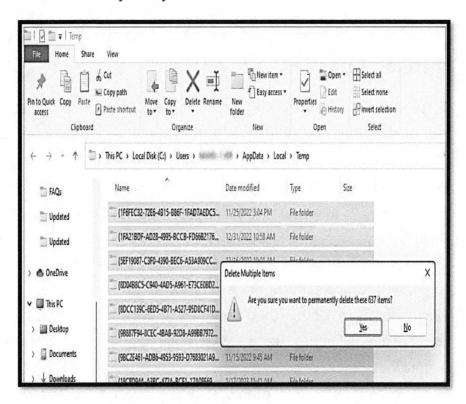

6. Run SFC Scan (System File Checker):

- Running an SFC scan can help identify and repair corrupted or damaged system files. This built-in Windows utility can be a valuable tool in resolving freezing problems.

7. Check Issues with RAM:

- Utilize the Windows Memory Diagnostic tool to check for RAM issues. Faulty or corrupted RAM can lead to system freezes. Running this tool can help diagnose and, if possible, repair RAM problems.

8. Reset Windows to Factory Settings:

- As a last resort, you can reset Windows 11 to its factory settings. However, be aware that this action will erase all apps, files, drivers, and customizations. Ensure you back up your important data before proceeding with a reset.

Broken Apps

Dealing with malfunctioning apps can be a source of frustration, as it can hinder both productivity and the overall user experience. Various factors, such as corrupt files, missing components, or compatibility issues, can contribute to these problems. Depending on the nature of the app and its source, different methods can be employed to resolve these issues.

One approach involves utilizing the Settings app, primarily designed for UWP (Universal Windows Platform) apps obtained from the Microsoft Store. Within the Advanced options for each app, you have the choice to either Repair or Reset the app, addressing issues accordingly.

For applications and programs acquired outside the Microsoft Store and directly installed on your computer, the Control Panel serves as a helpful tool. In this case, you can navigate to Programs and Features, where you'll find the option to Repair or Change each program, aiding in troubleshooting and repair.

A more advanced method involves the use of the Command Prompt, which necessitates identifying the app's GUID (Globally Unique Identifier) and employing Windows Installer (MSIExec) commands to rectify issues. It's worth noting that this method requires a certain level of technical proficiency and caution.

Desktop keeps crashing

Your desktop may experience frequent crashes due to various potential causes. Here are some common factors:

1. Corrupted System Files: When system files become corrupt or damaged, Windows may malfunction. Utilize tools like SFC (System File Checker) or DISM (Deployment Image Servicing and Management) to attempt repairs.

2. Outdated or Incompatible Drivers: Out-of-date or incompatible drivers can lead to hardware or software conflicts. Keep your drivers up-to-date through Windows Update, Device Manager, or manufacturer websites.

3. Malware or Virus Infections: Malicious software can compromise your system files and processes. Safeguard your computer by scanning it with Windows Defender or a trusted third-party antivirus program to remove any detected threats.

4. Overheating: Excessive heat can cause CPU, GPU, or other component malfunctions. Monitor temperatures using tools like HWMonitor or SpeedFan and ensure proper ventilation and cooling for your PC.

5. Faulty or Incompatible Hardware: Incompatible or faulty hardware components can introduce instability. Inspect your RAM, storage drive, power supply, and peripherals for issues, and consider replacement if necessary.

6. Conflicting Applications: Certain applications may conflict with Windows or other software. Uninstall recently added or suspicious apps and investigate compatibility with Windows 11.

7. Damaged or Corrupted Registry: The registry stores crucial settings and information for Windows and applications. Safely clean and repair your registry with tools like CCleaner or Registry Editor, but exercise caution to avoid unintended modifications.

8. Hardware Problems: Flawed hardware components, such as malfunctioning RAM, a problematic hard drive, or an overheating CPU, can result in system crashes.

Error Types

In Windows 11, various types of errors can occur, each with its source and level of severity. Here are some common error categories:

1. BSOD (Blue Screen of Death) Error Codes: BSOD errors manifest as hexadecimal codes on a blue screen when Windows encounters a critical system error leading to a system crash. These codes aid in pinpointing the root cause of the crash, whether it's a faulty hardware component, a corrupted driver, or a malware infection. For example, CRITICAL_PROCESS_DIED indicates that a vital system process terminated unexpectedly, while IRQL_NOT_LESS_OR_EQUAL suggests that a kernel-mode process or driver attempted to access a memory address without proper authorization. You can reference a comprehensive list of BSOD error codes and their explanations in this article.

2. Application Error Codes: These codes, whether numeric or textual, convey the status of an application or a specific operation within it. They prove useful in troubleshooting software-related issues or compatibility challenges. For instance, 0x80070002 signifies The system cannot find the file specified, and 0xC0000005 indicates an Access violation. You can access a comprehensive list of application error codes and their meanings in this article.

3. Device Manager Error Codes: These are numeric codes that convey the status of a device or its associated driver. They are valuable for diagnosing hardware problems or driver conflicts.

How to find your error code in Device Manager

- Double-click the device category experiencing problems.
- Right-click the specific problematic device, and select Properties. This action will open the Properties dialog box for the device, where you can locate the error code in the Device status section.

Error Codes and Their Resolutions

1. Error Code 1: This device is not configured correctly. (Code 1)

Cause: This error occurs when the device lacks proper drivers on your computer, or the existing drivers are configured incorrectly.

Recommended Resolution: To resolve this issue, follow these steps:

Update the Driver:

- In the device's Properties dialog box, navigate to the Driver tab.
- Click Update Driver to initiate the Hardware Update Wizard.
- Follow the on-screen instructions to update the driver.

Consult Hardware Documentation:

- If updating the driver doesn't resolve the problem, consult the documentation provided with your hardware for more specific guidance.

By following these steps, you can address Error Code 1 and ensure that the device is configured correctly.

2. Error Code 3: The driver for this device might be corrupted

Full error message: The driver for this device might be corrupted, or your system may be running low on memory or other resources. (Code 3)

Cause: This error occurs due to one of two potential reasons:

- The device driver may be corrupted.
- Your system is running low on memory or other essential resources.

Recommended Resolutions:

1. Close Some Open Applications:

- If your computer lacks sufficient memory to operate the device, you can free up memory by closing some applications.
- Additionally, you should check the system's memory and resource usage.

To check memory and system resources:

- Open Task Manager by pressing CTRL+ALT+DELETE and then clicking on Task Manager.

2. Review Virtual Memory Settings:

- To assess virtual memory settings, follow these steps:
  - Open the System Properties dialog box.
  - Click on the Advanced tab.
  - In the Performance area, click on Settings.

3. Error Code 9: Windows cannot identify this hardware

Full error message: Windows cannot identify this hardware because it does not have a valid hardware identification number. For assistance, contact the hardware manufacturer. (Code 9)

Cause: This error occurs when your PC detects invalid device identification numbers associated with your hardware.

Recommended Resolutions: To resolve this issue, follow these steps:

1. Contact the Hardware Vendor:

- Reach out to the hardware manufacturer for assistance.
- This error may indicate a hardware or driver defect that requires their attention and support.

4. Error Code 10: This device cannot start.

Full Error Message: This device cannot start. Try upgrading the device drivers for this device.

Cause: Usually, the device's hardware key contains a FailReasonString value, and the displayed error message is defined by the hardware manufacturer within this value. If the hardware key does not contain a FailReasonString value, the message above is displayed.

Recommended Resolutions: To resolve this issue, follow these steps:

Update the driver:

- Open the device's Properties dialog box.
- Click on the Driver tab.
- Click the Update Driver button to initiate the Hardware Update Wizard.
- Follow the on-screen instructions to update the driver for the device.

5. Error Code 14: This device cannot work properly until you restart your computer.

Full error message: This device cannot work properly until you restart your computer. To restart your computer now, click Restart Computer. (Code 14)

Recommended Resolution: To resolve this issue, follow these steps:

1. Restart Your Computer:

- Click on the Start menu.
- Select Shut Down.
- Choose Restart to initiate the computer restart process.

6. Error Code 16: Windows cannot identify all the resources this device uses.

Full error message: Windows cannot identify all the resources this device uses. To specify additional resources for this device, click the Resources tab and fill in the missing settings. Check your hardware documentation to find out what settings to use. (Code 16)

Cause: This error occurs when the device is only partially configured, and additional manual configuration of the required resources for the device is necessary.

Recommended Resolution: To resolve this issue, please follow these steps:

1. Access Device Manager:
- Click on the Start menu.
- Search for Device Manager and select it from the search results.

2. Configure Resources:
- Double-click on the device listed in Device Manager.

3. Access the Resources Tab:
- Click on the Resources tab in the device's Properties dialog box.

4. Check for Missing Resources:
- In the Resource Settings list, check if there is a question mark next to any resource. If you find a resource with a question mark, it indicates that it needs to be assigned to the device.

5. Assign Resources:
- Select the resource with the question mark and assign it to the device.

6. Change Settings if Needed:

- If a resource cannot be changed, click on Change Settings. If the Change Settings option is unavailable, try clearing the Use automatic settings check box to make it available.

7. Error Code 18: Reinstall the drivers for this device.

Recommended Resolutions:

1. Reinstall the Device Driver using the Hardware Update Wizard:
- Click on the Start menu.
- Search for Device Manager and select it from the search results.
- Right-click on the device listed in Device Manager.
- From the menu that appears, choose Update Driver to initiate the Hardware Update wizard.

2. Reinstall the Device Driver Manually:
- Click on the Start menu.
- Search for Device Manager and select it from the search results.
- Right-click on the device listed in Device Manager.
- Select Uninstall from the menu that appears.
- After the device is uninstalled, choose Action on the menu bar.
- Select Scan for hardware changes to reinstall the driver.

8. Error Code 21: Windows is removing this device.

Full error message: Windows is removing this device.

Cause: This error indicates that Windows is currently in the process of removing a device, but the removal procedure hasn't been completed yet. It's a temporary error that occurs during attempts to query and remove a device.

Recommended Resolutions:

To resolve this issue, consider the following steps:

1. Wait for Windows to Complete the Removal:

- First, exercise patience and allow Windows to finish the removal process. The error is often temporary and will resolve itself when the removal is complete.

2. Refresh the Device Manager View:

- If the problem persists, wait for a few seconds, and then press the F5 key to refresh the Device Manager view. This can help ensure that the removal process has been successfully executed.

3. Restart Your Computer:

- If waiting and refreshing do not resolve the problem, consider restarting your computer.
- Click on the Start menu.
- Select Shut Down.
- Choose Restart in the Shut Down Windows dialog box to initiate the computer restart process.

9. Error Code 22: This device is disabled.

Cause: This error occurs when the user has intentionally disabled the device in Device Manager.

Recommended Resolution: To resolve this issue and enable the device, follow these steps:

1. Open Device Manager.
2. Click on the Action menu.
3. Select Enable Device. This action will initiate the Enable Device wizard.
4. Follow the on-screen instructions provided by the wizard to enable the device.

10. Error Code 44: An application or service has shut down this hardware device.

Recommended Resolution: To resolve this issue, follow these steps:

1. Restart Your Computer:

- Click on the Start menu.
- Select Shut Down.
- Choose Restart from the Shut Down Windows dialog box to initiate the computer restart process.

11. Error Code 54: This device has failed and is undergoing a reset.
Cause: Error Code 54 is assigned when there's an intermittent problem with a device, typically during the execution of an ACPI reset method. If the device fails to restart properly, it can remain in this state, necessitating a system reboot.
Recommended Resolution: To resolve this issue, follow these steps:
1. Restart Your Computer:
- Click on the Start menu.
- Select Shut Down.
- Choose Restart from the Shut Down Windows dialog box to initiate the computer restart process.

Windows blue screen of death (BSOD)

The Blue Screen of Death (BSOD) serves as a diagnostic tool for identifying hardware and memory faults. It's an error and bug-check mechanism within Windows that provides administrators with valuable data to analyze the root cause of the system issue leading to the blue screen. So, when your computer encounters a blue screen, there's no need to panic. A blue error screen emerges when your computer faces a severe issue. This problem can be triggered by various factors, including low-level software crashes (such as drivers) and malfunctioning hardware components. Typically, the BSOD displays an error code and description directly on the screen, enabling you to seek relevant assistance by either scanning the code or searching for information.

When your computer encounters a critical problem, it initiates an abrupt restart to safeguard your system from potential damage. It's worth noting that some users might encounter a black screen in Windows 11 instead of the traditional blue one. This is essentially the same issue, with the distinction that it may occur on older versions of Windows 11.

Troubleshooting Windows 11 Blue Screen of Death (BSOD)

 Microsoft acknowledged the occurrence of the Blue Screen of Death (BSOD) and other issues in Windows 11, the new operating system. These problems include BSOD triggered by compatibility issues with Intel drivers, Microsoft Installer (MSI) failures affecting app updates or repairs, and more.

Quick Fix: Restart Your Computer When faced with the BSOD, the initial instinct is often to restart the computer, hoping to resolve the issue. Upon restarting, Windows 11 initiates an automatic troubleshooting and repair process, often leading to a return to normalcy after a simple restart when encountering problems like the BSOD.

Tips: Stop Automatic Reboot after Blue Screen Errors If you wish to prevent your Windows 11 computer from automatically rebooting after a BSOD, follow these steps:

1. Press Win + I to open the Settings window.

2. Navigate to System > Advanced system settings.

3. Click on the Settings button in the Startup and Recovery section.

4. Locate the System failure section and uncheck Automatically restart.

5. Click OK to save the changes.

Whenever a BSOD appears on your computer, take note of the error code and allow Windows to automatically address the problem by rebooting the computer.

However, restarting may not always work, as some users have reported that the problem persists even after rebooting Windows 11. In such cases, consider the following fixes:

Fix 1: Disconnect Unnecessary Devices Check if your computer is connected to external devices. If so, disconnect them all and then restart your computer. Some external devices can interfere with the computer's boot process, potentially causing a BSOD.

Fix 2: Reboot in Safe Mode If the BSOD prevents normal computer use, accessing Safe Mode is advisable. Safe Mode allows your computer to operate with basic configurations, without running third-party software, helping diagnose potential system issues.

- To enter Safe Mode when your computer cannot boot normally due to a BSOD:

- Press the Power button and hold it for at least 10 seconds to turn off your computer.

- Turn the computer back on by pressing the Power button again. Repeat this process several times until you see the Windows logo or messages like Please wait or Diagnosing your PC.

- Click on Advanced options to enter the Choose an option window.

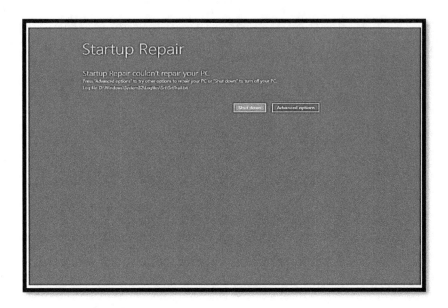

- Select Troubleshoot > Advanced options > Startup Settings > Restart.
- Press F4 to Enable Safe Mode or F5 to Enable Safe Mode with Networking.

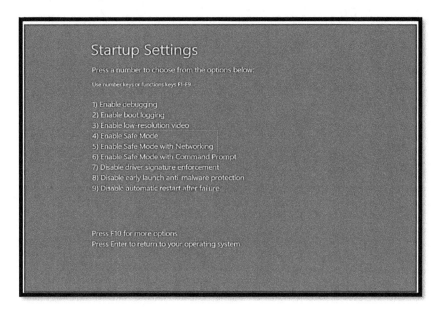

Fix 3: Uninstall Third-party Software If you've recently installed third-party software before experiencing a BSOD, that software may be the culprit. You can uninstall it after restarting or while in Safe Mode.

- To uninstall third-party software:
- Click Start and select Settings.
- Go to Apps > Apps & features.
- Browse the installed software list.
- Select the recently added third-party software or any software you suspect is causing the issue.
- Click Uninstall and wait.
- Restart your computer.

Fix 4: Uninstall Recent Updates This method is particularly effective if the BSOD occurs after a recent Windows 11 update.

- To uninstall recent updates (in Safe Mode):
- Open Settings > Windows Update > Update history.
- Click Uninstall Updates under Related settings.
- Browse the list and select the most recent updates.
- Right-click to choose Uninstall.

Fix 5: Rebuild the Master Boot Record (MBR)

The Master Boot Record (MBR) is a critical component that determines the location and method of accessing an operating system. If the MBR becomes corrupted, your computer may become unresponsive and stuck on the blue screen during startup. Here are two methods to repair the MBR and restore your device's boot functionality.

Using the Command Prompt Tool:

Step 1: Access the Windows Repair Environment by restarting your computer and holding down the Shift key.

Step 2: In the Choose an option window, navigate to Troubleshoot > Advanced options > Command Prompt.

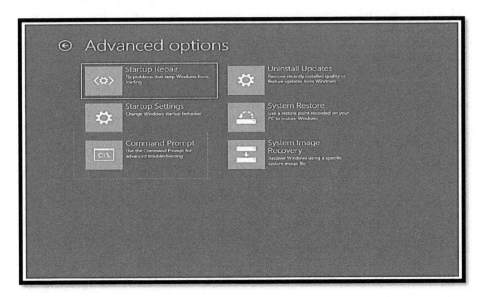

Step 3: Once in the Command Prompt, enter the following commands one by one, pressing Enter after each:

- **bootrec /Fixmbr**
- **bootrec /FixBoot**
- **bootrec /ScanOs**
- **bootrec /RebuildBcd**

Step 4: After running these commands, type **exit** to close the Command Prompt window.

Step 5: Restart your computer to see if the MBR has been successfully repaired and if the issue with the blue screen is resolved.

What to Do When Your Computer Works Normally Again

If your computer functions properly after an automatic restart, you can take the following steps to prevent the recurrence of a blue screen issue.

Method 1: Update/Rollback/Disable/Uninstall Drivers

1. Press the Windows key + X.
2. Select Device Manager.
3. Expand the category of a device that you suspect has problematic drivers.
4. Right-click on the driver you wish to address and choose Properties.
5. Go to the Driver tab.
6. Depending on your needs, click on Update Driver, Roll Back Driver, Disable Device, or Uninstall Device.
7. Follow the on-screen instructions to proceed.

Method 2: Run the Windows Memory Diagnostic Tool If you encounter a Memory Management blue screen error, which is often associated with RAM issues, it's advisable to diagnose the RAM's health using the Windows Memory Diagnostic Tool before considering a replacement.

1. Press the Windows key + S to open the Search bar.
2. Type Windows Memory Diagnostic and press Enter.
3. Select Restart now and check for problems (recommended).
4. Allow the tool to perform the memory test.
5. If it identifies an issue with your memory, you may need to replace the RAM.

6. You can also review the most recent Memory Diagnostic file by opening Event Viewer, selecting Windows Logs, and clicking System.

Method 3: Scan the Hard Drive for Errors Aside from memory errors, a faulty hard drive can also trigger BSOD. You can check for hard drive issues and address them using one of the following methods:

Using Error Checking:

1. Press the Windows key + E.

2. Navigate to This PC > Local Disk (C:) > Properties > Tool.

3. Click on the Check button under the Error-checking section.

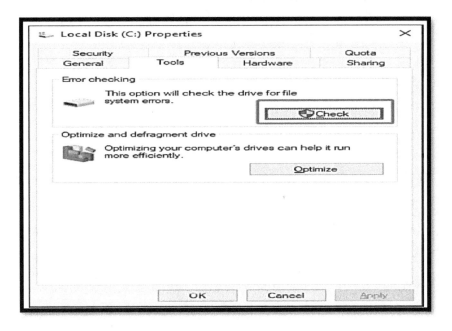

4. Follow the on-screen instructions.

Method 4: Perform an SFC Scan If you encounter a CRITICAL_PROCESS_DIED blue screen error, you can utilize the System File Checker (SFC) tool to repair missing or corrupted system files.

1. Press Win + R to open the Run window and press Ctrl + Shift + Enter to run the command prompt as an administrator.
2. Type SFC/scan now and click on Enter.

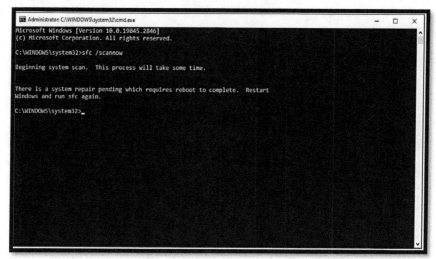

3. Allow the command to complete.

Method 5: Scan Your Computer for Viruses or Malware Virus or malware attacks can lead to blue screen issues. To determine if your computer is affected, you can use Windows Security's Virus & Threat Protection feature to scan and remove any threats.

1. Press the Windows key + S.
2. Type Windows Security and press Enter.
3. Select Virus & Threat Protection> Scan options.
4. Choose the desired scan type.

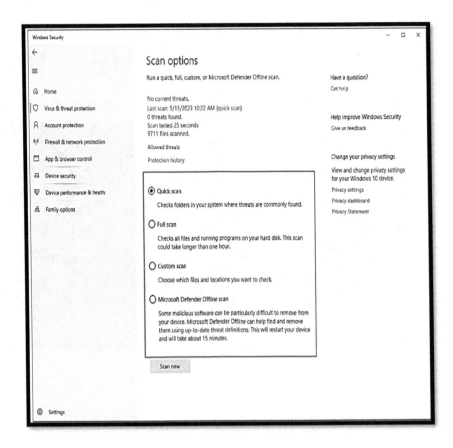

5. Follow the on-screen instructions to remove any detected viruses or malware.

Recovering Lost Data from Your Computer

A blue screen event can lead to data loss, even if your computer appears to be functioning normally after a restart. If you find yourself in this situation, we recommend using MiniTool Power Data Recovery, a robust and free data recovery software that can help you retrieve your lost data in various scenarios.

MiniTool Power Data Recovery offers the ability to check if a scanned partition contains the files you're looking for and allows you to recover up to 1 GB of data for free. With its user-friendly design, you can efficiently locate and recover your desired files. Follow these steps to check for lost data and recover your files:

Step 1: Download and install MiniTool Power Data Recovery.

Step 2: Launch the software and select the drive where your lost data was stored.

Step 3: Click the Scan button and wait for the scanning process to complete.

Step 4: Browse through the scan results and select the files you want to recover. You can use the Preview button to review them.

Step 5: Click the Save button and choose a storage location for your recovered files.

Step 6: Confirm your selection by clicking OK and wait for all the items to be fully recovered.

By following these steps, you can use MiniTool Power Data Recovery to retrieve your lost data efficiently and effectively.

How to fix bluescreens (BSOD)

Using Task Manager and Ctrl-Alt-Del

1. Press Control + Alt + Del: This keyboard shortcut is commonly used to access a menu of options in Windows, including Task Manager. When you press these keys simultaneously, it brings up the Security Options screen.

2. Click Task Manager: On the Security Options screen, you will see a list of options and one of them is Task Manager. Clicking on it will open the Windows Task Manager.

3. Click the Details tab: The Windows Task Manager typically opens with the Processes tab selected, but in this step, you are instructed to switch to the Details tab. The Details tab provides more detailed information about running processes and applications.

4. Select wininit.exe: In the Details tab, you'll see a list of all the processes running on your computer. These processes are essential for the functioning of your operating system and installed applications. wininit.exe is a crucial Windows system process responsible for system initialization tasks. In some cases, you may want to end this process to initiate a system restart.

5. Click End task: After selecting the wininit.exe process, you can click the End task button. Ending a task in Task Manager forcibly terminates the selected process. In the case of wininit.exe, this action will likely initiate a system shutdown or restart. Be cautious when ending tasks, as terminating critical system processes can lead to instability or data loss if unsaved work is present.

6. Follow the on-screen shutdown: After ending the task, your computer should respond by initiating the shutdown process or displaying a dialog box confirming your intention to shut down or restart. Follow the on-screen prompts to complete the shutdown.

System configuration Utility (MSCONFIG)

The System Configuration Utility, commonly known as MSCONFIG, serves as a valuable tool for users. It enables you to make adjustments to a range of settings that pertain to your system's startup and overall performance. With MSCONFIG, you can address problems arising from conflicting programs, services, or drivers. Additionally, it provides the means to enhance your system's efficiency by deactivating superfluous items that initiate during startup.

To access MSConfig follow these steps:

1. Click on the magnifying glass icon located on the Windows taskbar.

2. In the text field at the top of the search window, type msconfig and then press the Enter key.

The System Configuration Utility window should now open and be ready for use.

It offers several features to help diagnose and optimize your computer's performance:

1. General/Startup Selection:

The default tab in the System Configuration utility is the General tab, which provides information about the computer's startup configuration. By default, the Normal startup option should be selected. However, if you've made changes to the settings in the Boot tab or disabled certain programs or services from starting up, the Selective Startup option will be automatically chosen. When the operating system is set to use Selective Startup, it will provide a reminder notification to inform you that this mode is currently active.

- **Normal:** Boots the system with all services and drivers, suitable for regular use.
- **Diagnostic:** Starts Windows with essential services and drivers to troubleshoot issues, excluding third-party services.
- **Selective:** Allows you to choose which services and programs start with Windows, enhancing startup speed and aiding in problem identification.

The Selective Startup mode helps diagnose startup problems by allowing you to enable items one at a time and observe system behavior.

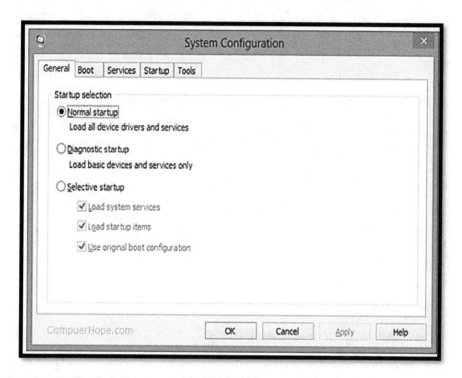

2. Boot Tab:

This tab offers you the ability to make adjustments to your system's startup settings, similar to the modifications you can make in the Windows boot.ini file, all without the need to directly edit the file. Moreover, you can fine-tune additional settings within the Advanced Options section, which includes options such as specifying the number of processors to utilize during boot, setting a maximum memory limit, and configuring various debugging options.

- **Safe Boot: Minimal:** Boots with critical services only, no networking.

- **Safe Boot: Alternate Shell:** Boots to a command prompt with critical services.
- **Safe Boot: Active Directory Repair:** Boots with critical services and Active Directory.
- **Safe Boot Network:** Boots with critical services and networking.
- **No GUI Boot:** Skips the Windows splash screen.
- **Boot Log:** Logs boot process information in ntbtlog.txt.
- **Base Video:** Uses standard VGA drivers for video troubleshooting.
- **OS Boot Information:** Displays driver loading during boot.
- **Make All Boot Settings Permanent:** Applies changes permanently.
- **Timeout Settings:** Configures countdown time for multi-boot systems.
- **Advanced Settings:** Allows configuration of processor count, memory, and debugging options (use with caution).

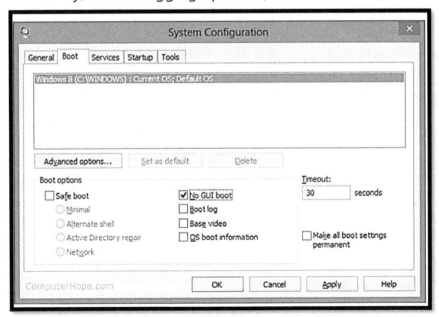

3. Services Tab

Within the Services tab, you can enable or disable various services that are part of Microsoft Windows or other program services currently active on your computer. To streamline your view and focus solely on non-Windows services, you can tick the Hide all Microsoft services box located at the bottom of the window. By unchecking a service's box, you effectively prevent it from initiating during startup.

- Lists services that start with the boot.
- Allows you to deselect services to troubleshoot issues.
- Changing services may switch the startup mode to Selective Startup.
- Exercise caution when disabling services; some are essential for system functionality.

4. Startup Tab

The Startup tab is often the primary destination for many Windows users when they access the System Configuration utility. Within this tab, you gain control over the initiation and termination of programs (also known as TSRs) that launch each time your computer starts. These startup programs frequently contribute to sluggish system startup and performance. To improve your computer's boot speed, you can simply uncheck the box next to any program you wish to prevent from starting automatically with each boot.

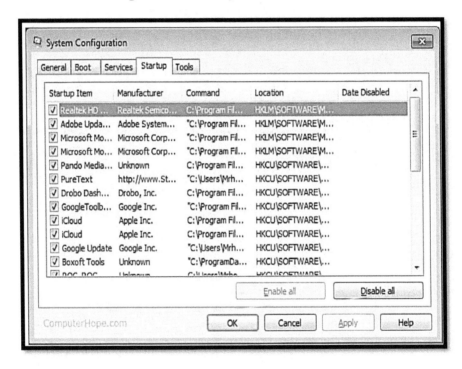

5. Tools Tab

The Tools tab offers convenient access to various Microsoft Windows tools. For instance, you can access the Event Viewer tool by choosing the Event Viewer option from the list of tools and then clicking on the Launch button.

- Provides a list of diagnostic and informational tools and their locations.
- Allows you to launch system tools directly or note their locations.
- Centralizes access to various tools and command-line options.
- Useful for system diagnostics and maintenance.

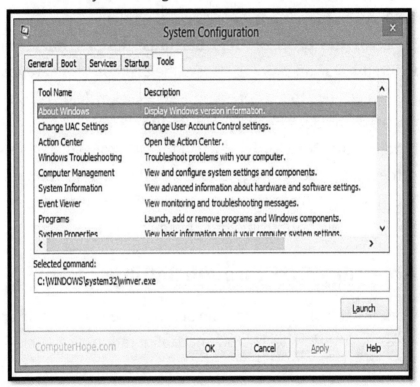

Booting with the Windows DVD to run repair Utilities

Booting from a Windows DVD to utilize repair utilities is a method to address common issues that may hinder your PC's startup or performance. Repair utilities encompass a range of tools designed to assist in restoring your system to a previous state, recovering files, diagnosing problems, and more.

To initiate the process of booting from a Windows DVD to access repair utilities, you should follow these steps:

1. Prepare an Installation DVD or USB Drive: To begin, ensure you have either a Windows 11 installation DVD or a bootable USB drive. You can create a bootable USB drive using the Media Creation Tool or obtain the ISO file from Microsoft's official website and then use a tool like Rufus to burn it onto a DVD or USB drive.

2. Access the BIOS or UEFI Settings: Restart your computer, and during the startup process, access the BIOS or UEFI settings. Typically, you can achieve this by pressing a specific key (e.g., F2, Del, or Esc) as indicated on your screen during startup.

3. Adjust the Boot Order: Within the BIOS or UEFI settings, navigate to the boot order configuration. Modify the boot order so that the DVD drive or USB drive is set as the primary boot option, ensuring that the system will boot from your chosen installation media.

Accessing BIOS through Settings

Accessing the BIOS through the Settings menu is a viable approach to accessing the low-level system configuration of your PC. BIOS, an acronym for Basic Input/Output System, serves as software responsible for managing your computer's hardware settings and boot sequence. It's worth noting that BIOS is sometimes referred to as UEFI, which stands for Unified Extensible Firmware Interface, representing a newer and more advanced iteration of the BIOS system.

To access the BIOS settings through the Settings app, follow these steps:

1. Open the Settings app by either pressing the Windows + I keys or clicking the Start button and selecting Settings.

2. In the Settings app, click on System located in the left sidebar.

3. Scroll down on the System page and find Recovery.

4. Within the Recovery section, under Recovery options, click on Restart Now next to Advanced Startup.

5. Your PC will restart, and you will see the Choose an option screen. Click on Troubleshoot.

6. On the Troubleshoot screen, select Advanced options.

7. In the Advanced options menu, click on UEFI Firmware Settings.

8. Your PC will prompt you to restart to modify UEFI firmware settings. Confirm by clicking Restart.

9. Your PC will reboot once more, entering the BIOS mode. Here, you can make adjustments to various hardware settings, configure the boot order, enhance security settings, and more.

Accessing BIOS using shift + restart

To access your BIOS using the Shift key during a restart, follow these steps:

1. While on the sign-in or lock screen, press the Shift key on your keyboard.

2. Simultaneously, tap on the power button (or click on the Power option located at the bottom right of your screen).

3. From the menu that appears, select the Restart option.

4. Windows 11 will initiate a restart, and you will be presented with the Advanced Startup screen, also known as the Choose an Option screen.

5. Navigate to Troubleshoot > Advanced options > UEFI Firmware Settings, and then click Restart.

6. Your computer will restart, entering the UEFI/BIOS mode. Here, you can access and configure various BIOS settings and preferences.

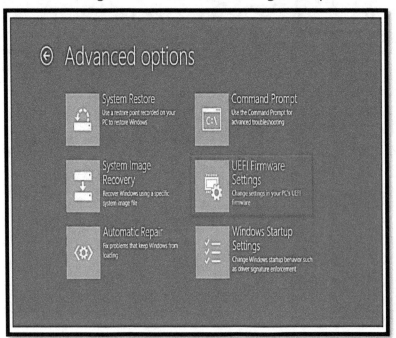

Accessing BIOS from the run Window

To access the BIOS via the Windows Run command, follow these steps:

1. Open the Run dialog by pressing the Windows key + R on your keyboard.

2. In the Run box, type shutdown /r /o and press Enter. Alternatively, for quicker access to your BIOS, you can type shutdown /r /o /f /t 00 and then click OK.

3. Your computer will initiate a restart.

4. Upon restarting, select Troubleshoot > Advanced options > UEFI Firmware Settings, and then press Restart.

5. Your computer will reboot and enter the system BIOS settings, allowing you to configure various BIOS options and settings.

CONCLUSION

Troubleshooting is an integral part of maintaining a smooth and reliable computing experience in Windows 11. While these issues can be frustrating, the operating system offers a suite of tools and resources to help users diagnose and resolve problems effectively. Staying informed about troubleshooting techniques and error messages empowers users to overcome common challenges and keep their systems running smoothly.

INDEX

338

Control Panel, 26, 31, 34, 35,
    36, 63, 64, 70, 71, 111, 184,
    186, 187, 286
copying, 101, 102, 113, 176
Cortana, 27, 28, 37, 109
Custom page layout, 119

D

Desktop, 2, 6, 29, 35, 36, 106,
    116, 142, 286
desktops, 2, 6, 81, 116
Device Manager, 75, 76, 78,
    292, 293
Domains, 180, 193
dual monitors, 81
Dynamic Host Configuration,
    181, 186

E

email, 31, 40, 44, 57, 144, 149,
    152, 157, 158, 159, 160, 161,
    162, 163, 164, 165, 166, 169,
    170, 171, 172, 173, 176, 178,
    179
Error Codes, 288, 289
Extensions and add-ons, 129

F

Facial recognition, 215
favorites,, 117, 118

File Explorer, 98, 99, 100, 101,
    102, 103, 104, 105, 106, 108,
    109, 111, 112, 113, 116, 117,
    177, 178, 220, 221, 222, 223,
    224, 225, 226, 283
files, 1, 5, 8, 10, 12, 16, 29, 32,
    39, 40, 45, 47, 60, 68, 87, 98,
    99, 101, 102, 103, 105, 107,
    108, 109, 111, 112, 113, 115,
    117, 118, 123, 144, 163, 164,
    171, 174, 175, 176, 178, 180,
    182, 189, 193, 194, 196, 207,
    213, 220, 221, 224, 225, 227,
    259, 260, 261,262, 278, 279,
    282, 284, 285, 286, 287, 302,
    304, 305, 312
folder, 13, 36, 88, 89, 98, 99,
    100, 101, 102, 103, 104, 105,
    106, 107, 108, 109, 110, 111,
    112, 120, 121, 128, 129, 166,
    167, 168, 169, 177, 178, 194,
    196, 197, 219, 220, 221, 223,
    226, 227, 234, 235, 236, 270,
    284

G

Gaming, 3, 146, 147, 240
gear-shaped icon, 63, 66, 70,
    150
Google account, 86, 171, 172
Google Chrome, 85, 86, 87

Groove Music, 260, 261

144, 195, 226, 246, 250, 251,
252, 254, 255, 257, 258, 260,
262

Microsoft Store, 4, 18, 30, 48,
90, 93, 95, 96, 97, 129, 143,
148, 204, 212, 236, 237, 238,
244, 245, 246, 247, 248, 249,
250, 251, 252, 253, 255, 256,
257, 258, 261, 286

Mouse pointer, 61, 62, 63, 72

Mouse Settings, 58, 67, 70

Moving,, 101

Music streaming, 258

N

native games, 146, 235, 236

Network, 50, 99, 140, 141, 156,
177, 182, 183, 184, 186, 187,
188, 189, 190, 191, 192, 262,
272, 273, 274, 277, 309

O

OneDrive, 40, 48, 99, 112, 115,
144, 164, 165, 195, 196, 197,
225, 226, 227

Outlook, 40, 115, 144, 157, 159,
160, 161, 162, 163, 164, 165,
166, 167, 175, 176

P

PC Health Check app, 9, 158

Personalization, 23, 29, 31, 35,
36, 82, 83, 141, 142, 169, 170

Photos app, 194, 195, 196, 197,
198, 199, 200, 201, 203, 211,
212, 218, 230, 231, 232, 233

R

reset disk, 46, 47

S

Scan, 80, 233, 234, 285, 293,
301, 302, 303, 304

scanner, 49, 50, 234

Screen savers, 31

Settings app, 23, 32, 37, 40, 44,
49, 51, 59, 61, 63, 66, 70, 73,
81, 86, 90, 92, 132, 134, 137,
138, 141, 145, 146, 153, 156,
178, 179, 182, 186, 188, 286,
313

slideshow, 30, 197, 200, 201,
202

Snap Assist,, 2

Snap feature, 2

Snapshot Group, 6

software, 19, 49, 57, 74, 75, 77,
87, 88, 92, 97, 112, 143, 151,

174, 178, 180, 195, 234, 264, 279, 282, 287, 288, 295, 297, 298, 299, 304, 313

sounds, 29, 30, 31

standard account, 39

Start button, 1, 22, 25, 27, 30, 31, 51, 57, 64, 132, 136, 137, 141, 145, 149, 155, 159, 246, 250, 257, 261, 313

Start menu, 1, 2, 5, 8, 20, 21, 22, 23, 24, 25, 29, 32, 44, 45, 59, 60, 66, 73, 78, 82, 111, 132, 137, 142, 149, 158, 159, 160, 161, 163, 164, 165, 167, 168, 169, 170, 182, 184, 187, 231, 235, 236, 237, 243, 245, 247, 249, 253, 262, 272, 274, 281, 291, 292, 293, 294, 295

storage device, 3, 10, 112, 218, 220, 222, 224

Switching user accounts, 45

T

taskbar, 1, 2, 5, 6, 7, 20, 22, 24, 25, 26, 34, 35, 37, 45, 46, 66, 76, 78, 82, 98, 116, 124, 135, 138, 139, 142, 144, 149, 158, 159, 160, 161, 163, 164, 165, 167, 168, 169, 174, 175, 176, 196, 197, 199, 201, 202, 228,

229, 233, 235, 237, 238, 243, 245, 247, 249,250, 262, 307

theme and color settings, 30

Time and Language Settings, 145

troubleshoot, 75, 139, 156, 265, 272, 307, 310

troubleshooter, 140, 265, 267, 268, 276

troubleshooting, 75, 76, 141, 264, 268, 286, 288, 296, 309, 316

TV series, 240, 257

U

USB drive, 10, 11, 12, 313

USB flash drive, 10, 11, 12, 46, 47, 218, 222

User accounts, 47, 144

V

VLC Media, 88, 261, 262, 263

W

wallpapers, 6, 30

webpage, 119, 120

websites, 12, 123, 125, 126, 127, 128, 144, 253, 287

WhatsApp, 93, 94, 226

Widgets, 5, 18, 22, 24

www.ingramcontent.com/pod-product-compliance
Lightning Source LLC
LaVergne TN
LVHW081514050326
832903LV00025B/1490